LEGENDS AND LORE
OF SLEEPY HOLLOW AND THE
HUDSON VALLEY

JONATHAN KRUK

THE
History
PRESS

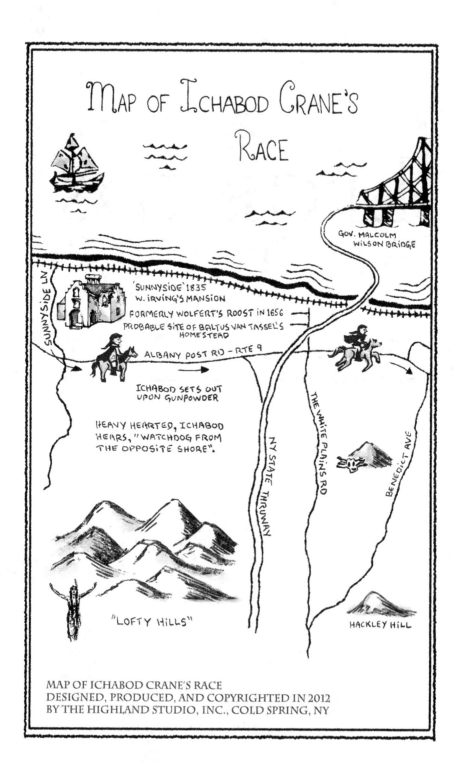

MAP OF ICHABOD CRANE'S RACE
DESIGNED, PRODUCED, AND COPYRIGHTED IN 2012
BY THE HIGHLAND STUDIO, INC., COLD SPRING, NY

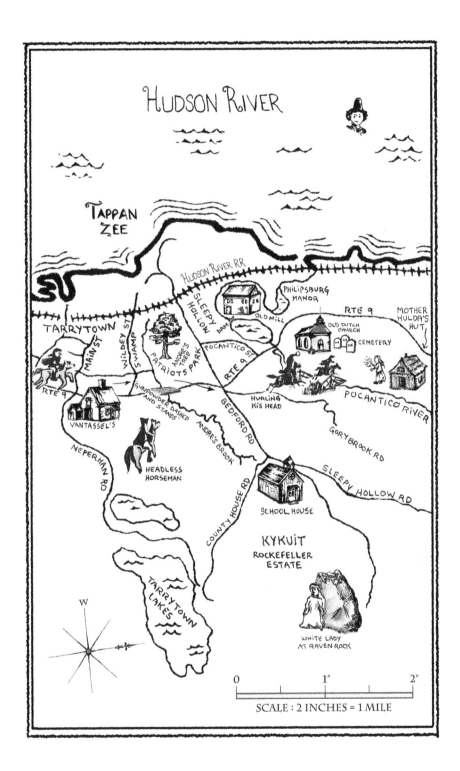

Published by The History Press
Charleston, SC   29403
www.historypress.net

Copyright © 2011 by Jonathan Kruk
All rights reserved

Front cover: *Headless Horseman in Pursuit of Ichabod Crane*, c. 1870. Watercolor on paper, Felix O.C. Darley. Historic Hudson Valley, Tarrytown, NY (ss.80.26). *Into Sleepy Hollow*, 2009 photograph, Todd Atteberry. www.thehistorytrekker.com.

First published 2011
Second printing 2012
Third printing 2013

ISBN 978.1.5402.2069.1

Library of Congress Cataloging-in-Publication Data

Kruk, Jonathan.
Legends and lore of Sleepy Hollow and the Hudson Valley / Jonathan Kruk.
p. cm.
Includes bibliographical references.
ISBN 978-1-5402-2069-1
1. Sleepy Hollow (N.Y.)--Social life and customs--Anecdotes. 2. Tarrytown (N.Y.)--Social life and customs--Anecdotes. 3. Hudson River Valley (N.Y. and N.J.)--Social life and customs--Anecdotes. 4. Irving, Washington, 1783-1859. Legend of Sleepy Hollow. 5. Legends--New York (State)--Sleepy Hollow. 6. Folklore--New York (State)--Sleepy Hollow. 7. Sleepy Hollow (N.Y.)--Biography--Anecdotes. I. Title.
F129.S682K78 2011
974.7'3--dc23
2011018252

CONTENTS

CONTENTS

PREFACE AND ACKNOWLEDGEMENTS

Who is the Headless Horseman of Sleepy Hollow? Why does he ride? Who are his kindred spirits and what are their stories? Where did Washington Irving find inspiration to write the Legend? *What's the local lore of the lower Hudson Valley?*

Curiosity chases the legendary Headless Horseman of Sleepy Hollow today. Thousands gather every October at the sites most associated with this gallivanting ghost. They seek, at Philipsburg Manor and nearby at the Old Dutch Church, an authentic and uniquely American experience of Halloween.

Performing in Sleepy Hollow since 1996, as Historic Hudson Valley's legend storyteller, people turn to me as an authority on the region's lore. Then they make me their confidant on the subject of its local ghosts. They pepper me with questions, offer theories and share encounters regarding a legend almost two hundred years old. This keen continuous interest motivated the research and story gathering for *Legends and Lore of Sleepy Hollow and the Hudson Valley.*

The Headless Horseman first galloped into our nightmares as a chapter collected into *The Sketch Book of Geoffrey Crayon, Gent.* by Washington Irving in 1819. Legends and letters tell us that this wayward New York lawyer living in England grew nostalgic for his boyhood ramblings through the moody mists of the lower Hudson Valley. Inspired by various sources, some oral, some written, the brooding Irving penned *The Legend of Sleepy Hollow.* A desire at the time for American stories launched the legend. A clever mix of characters and a little romance, culminating with a ghostly chase, from the new nation turned this tale into a tradition for telling and retelling.

The Legend inspired books, plays, ballets, a half dozen major films, haunted hayrides and countless place names. Indeed, myriad sources moved Washington Irving to create his classic. Heartbreak over the death of his beloved Matilda Hoffman prompted *The Legend*'s plot. Further, it brought the lovelorn Irving to Jesse Merwin. A New England schoolteacher in the Hudson Valley, Merwin shared his personal experience of an old Dutch American custom. This revelation, along with a quick entry in a Revolutionary War officer's journal, became the core of truth of *The Legend*. Detailed conversations with the descendants of New Netherlanders, including their servants and slaves, gave life to *The Legend*'s convincing characters.

Irving also enlivened his legend with elements found in German folklore. The biggest piece came from an old epic poem retold by Wilhelm Burger. Add a dash from Robert Burns, plus boundless imagination, and *The Legend* lives.

Washington Irving mentions and alludes to other ghosts of Sleepy Hollow. They haunt people too. When the crowd thins after a show, some tarry like the young Washington Irving did in Van Tassel's Tarrytown tavern, once just down the Old Albany Post Road from Philipsburg. Curious, they call out for more about the valley's spirits: "Who is this White Lady of Raven Rock?" "Have you heard of the witch, Mother Hulda?" "How do you stop Major Andre's ghost?" "Why do skippers shorten their sails for Hudson River imps?" "Does the Headless Hessian gallop through Scarsdale?"

The Headless Horseman truly dominates those other spirits of the region. Let them escape from beneath the big ghost's cloak, and each one delivers a gripping tale. This book also gives the fateful story of Major John Andre's ghost. I unearthed not just one but several White Ladies wailing warnings at Raven Rock. The origins of Sleepy Hollow's curse in Native American lore are illuminated here too.

The Legend of Sleepy Hollow's characters have provoked questions and claims as to who was the original. A former president of the United States even certified an acquaintance of his as a model for Irving. I address the genesis of Ichabod Crane, Katrina van Tassel, Brom Bones and Balt van Tassel.

The storied Hudson River provides a rich source of influence over Sleepy Hollow. People once feared river spirits called imps making mischief or wreaking havoc upon their sloops on the Hudson. Related tales of phantom ships and Revolutionary-era ghosts no doubt filled the head of the rambling Irving. The folklore given here of these spirits and some their history serves to complete this book. Finally, recent encounters with the supernatural are brought out to help illustrate Sleepy Hollow's continued sway over the land.

People looking for answers on the lore of *The Legend of Sleepy Hollow* will find Washington Irving charmingly circumspect. He triply distanced himself from the sources of the Headless Horseman. *The Legend*'s stated author, "Geoffrey Crayon," declares he found the story "among the papers of the late Diedrich Knickerbocker" (*TLSH*, 1).* This Dutch New Yorker goes on to proclaim he heard the tale from "a pleasant shabby, gentlemanly old fellow" (*TLSH*, postscript).

Further, when the gathering of Manhattan's "most sagest and illustrious burghers" listened to that gentleman spin his yarn, they questioned the veracity of *The Legend*. The storyteller confessed: "Faith sir, I don't believe the half of it myself!" People today, however, still persist in believing in the other half. They tend to agree with wise women of Sleepy Hollow, "the best judges of these matters" (*TLSH*, 74); supernatural spirits, they assert, abound in Sleepy Hollow!

The Legend offers more than Washington Irving's imaginative twists and romantic turns. There's a surfeit of stories here waiting to be told. Gathered into this book are the origins of the Headless Horseman, the stories of other Sleepy Hollow spirits, with the history and local folklore. My research uncovered facts most likely known but obscured by Washington Irving. The reenactor who often portrays the Headless Horseman at Historic Hudson Valley's *Legend* event led me to a West Point professor with proof of a Hessian decapitated at a battle Irving calls "nameless." Reconstructing the events leading to this moment, I put forth at the heart of this book a plausible account for the galloping Hessian's demise.

This decapitated specter rides on into our new millennium. In 1999, Tim Burton turned *The Legend* into a gory intrigue, with Johnny Depp playing Ichabod Crane as a detective. The Headless Horseman exists as a worldwide icon. Exploring his origins and revealing the spirits he presides over in the region made for a worthy endeavor for this contemporary taleteller. I am grateful to The History Press, and specifically my commissioning editor, Whitney Tarella, for taking on this project.

My quest for the source and stories surrounding the Headless Horseman took many twists and turns. First came all the queries from my audiences. I delved into over one hundred books. Next came the consultations with diverse experts: historical reenactors, interpreters, professors, linguists, longtime residents, mentors, seers and even blogging oracles. I attempted to unravel fact from fiction, but *The Legend of Sleepy Hollow* remains steadfast in keeping its secrets. Now, setting out in pursuit of that galloping Hessian and his hosts, I begin by sending forth my acknowledgements to those who helped on this endeavor.

---

* Please note that all quotes attributed to Washington Irving's *The Legend of Sleepy Hollow* will appear within the text with a paragraph number (*TLSH*, 1). The very short unattributed quotes are also from *The Legend*.

My deep gratitude goes to: my mentor, He Who Stands Firm, for sparking my interest in local lore; Todd Atteberry, photographer extraordinaire, who accompanied me on several legs of the journey; and Professor Boria Sax, who led me to the delightful Elisabeth Paling Funk, a rigorous scholar of the Dutch Americans and Irving. I am most thankful to all at Historic Hudson Valley: the late Charlie Duda, Russell Hubbard, Thom Thatcher, Rob Yasinsac, Kate Johnson, Catalina Hannan and Jessa Krick. Special thanks for the image expertise of Joe and Lisa Dieboll at the Highland Studio. I appreciate Mindy Krazmien and Kendall Ingenito at the Putnam County Historical Society, Sara Mascia at the Historical Society, Inc., serving Sleepy Hollow and Tarrytown and the Columbia County Historical Society. A special thanks goes to Neil Zuckerman, the DeSilvias and Don Troiani for use of their paintings, as well as Bryan Haeffele for his Headless Horseman photo. I salute Lieutenant Colonel Frank Licameli and Hugh Francis for helping me locate the original lost head. Carrie Katz, I am glad for your motivation. Huzzahs to Dickon Love, tower keeper of St. Magnus the Martyr in London; John Kand for tales of Major Andre; and to the Hessian reenactors John Lopez and Robert Sulentic. Thanks to Carol Donick; the staff at the Desmond Fish Library in Garrison, New York; the Julia Butterfield Library in Cold Spring, New York; Warner Library in Tarrytown, New York; Montclair Library in New Jersey; and the Liburnes at Antipodean Books, Garrison's Landing, New York. "En-na-shee" to Evan Pritchard for his help on Native American lore and to David M. Oestreicher for his counterpoint assistance. Thanks too for encouragement from Rich Bala, Kim Conner, Melissa Heckler, Alicia Kruk, Dorothy McTaggart and all the schoolchildren who urged me to write this book. I'm grateful to Zosia Kruk for turning a stack of books into a bibliography. Finally, I offer a heartfelt thanks to Andrea Sadler, my wife, for her boundless support.

My editors reminded me, while "collating and collecting," that people want the facts found in these legends and folklore to tell a story. I write then not as a scholar or a historian but as your storyteller. I leap into this book, mindful of the sage advice given by the renowned Alabama storyteller Kathryn Tucker Windham. When asked which spooky tales we should tell, Kate declared, "The only ghost stories worth telling are ones that are true." I agree!

Summary

WASHINGTON IRVING'S
THE LEGEND OF SLEEPY HOLLOW

Everyone knows Washington Irving's Headless Horseman. When people plunge into his twelve-thousand-word "short" story, they occasionally become "sorely puzzled by the ratiocination of the syllogism" (*TLSH*, postscript). Some folks grow impatient with Irving's clever circumlocution, thus failing to get to the ghostly finale. Here then is a summary, about one-tenth the length of *The Legend of Sleepy Hollow*.

Along the cove where the Hudson dances into the Pocantico, there wandered an itinerant schoolmaster from Connecticut. Looking like a scarecrow who had escaped his post, with a pointy snipe of nose, Ichabod Crane was most aptly named. He took on the job of schoolmaster in Sleepy Hollow. Living for a couple of weeks at a time in each of his young scholars' homes, he brought learning and a gazette of gossip into the gloomy community. By day, he used the birch branch to "urge tardy loiterers down the flowery path of knowledge." By night he sought students with good cooks for mothers, for he enjoyed the comforts of the cupboards. Above all, in the Hollow known for its ghost lore, Ichabod found no story detail too gory to hear. Soon, the schoolmaster fell under two spells.

First, the drowsy dreamy air of Sleepy Hollow enchanted Crane to sense spirits. The whole region abounds with haunted houses, haunted streams, bewitched barns and bridges. There appears in Sleepy Hollow the specter of Major Andre, the Revolutionary War spy. And one hears the moans of a mysterious Woman in White, wailing before storms sweep across the Tappan Zee.

The principal goblin and dominant spirit is that of a Headless Horseman. A cannonball carried away his head at an unnamed battle for independence, leaving a ghoulish ghost relentlessly seeking what he lost. The farm wives frightened the schoolmaster with fireside tales of this specter whom they called the galloping Hessian of Sleepy Hollow.

The other spell beguiled Ichabod more than any ghost, goblin or coven of witches. 'Twas that of a coquettish woman! Katrina van Tassel was a ripe, blooming lass known not only for her beauty but for the bounty anyone marrying her would inherit. She was the only daughter of Baltus van Tassel, the most prosperous farmer in the Hollow.

Ichabod courted Katrina as her singing master. He rolled his eyes over all the Van Tassels' abundant wheat fields and fruit orchards, imagining, "one day, all this will be mine." The course, of course, to true love, as the bard said, is never straight. Ichabod's route to Katrina was more crooked than a barrel of eels. Standing between Crane and Katrina was a "burly, roaring, roistering blade" known as Brom Bones. A Herculean figure, he rode like a Cossack through the Hollow and presented a ready rival to the scarecrow of a schoolmaster. Brom, though, made more of mischief than malice, threatening to "double the schoolmaster up, and lay him on a shelf!"

Clever Crane never agreed to meet his challenger on the open field for a round of fisticuffs. Heavens no! This forced Brawny Bones to turn to a charivari of tricks. He tried smoking Crane out of his school and even set a witch's web of booby traps. He trained a ridiculous dog to howl whenever Ichabod gave the Van Tassel heiress her singing lesson. Crane still would not give up his suit for Katrina!

Finally things come to a head, lest they'd go on this way too long. The Van Tassels held an annual autumnal "quilting frolic." Upon receiving the invitation, Ichabod cried, "School's dismissed!" Hair queued in an eel-skin, neck stock and knee britches, he got himself all dressed up. Then he borrowed for his knightly courting a sway-backed ornery plow horse named Gunpowder. Crane, with a love poem in his frock coat pocket, rode off to woo and win Katrina after the ball.

Again, passing by the Van Tassel farmstead, Ichabod imagined everything, complete with cooked ducks swimming to him in their own gravy, as "all mine." The Sleepy Hollow folk, decked out in brass buttons and ribbons, sat down together for the feast. Ichabod, though "exceedingly lank," had the "dilating powers of an anaconda." He ate with the joy other men felt for a good smoke or a strong drink.

When the ancient fiddler struck his bow, the schoolmaster bounced onto the dance floor. Every part of his lanky frame moving, he jittered and figured liked St. Vitus, the patron of the dance! Why this jumping with joy? Why, his partner was the desired Katrina van Tassel. The entire party watched, clapped and urged on Ichabod, while the great Brom Bones sulked. He was one of those men who believed dancing unmanly.

When the tune ended, Brom set his plan to work. He flattered and cajoled the veterans into polishing up their old Revolutionary War stories. Tales of sword and cannon inevitably led to stories of Sleepy Hollow's spirits. Talk turned to Farmer Brouwer. Right after he claimed, "I am a heretical disbeliever in ghosts!" the galloping Hessian bashed his brains. Brom followed with a frightful tale of his remarkable race with the Headless Horseman. Ichabod gasped when learning "the goblin rider vanished in a flash of fire." He cannot cross the bridge by the Old Dutch Church graveyard.

"Good night to all!" Baltus broke up revelry, and all merrily rode home. Ichabod approached Katrina like Romeo but soon returned to Gunpowder crestfallen. The coquette had led him on only to send him away.

The night along the Hudson looked as lonely as the rejected Master Crane. The forlorn schoolmaster felt the crickets and owls turn into spooks and spirits. Riding in fits and starts on the cantankerous horse, soon every blazed branch and forest creaking became an uncouth ghoul or the White Lady's ghost. Near the haunts of Wiley's swamp, Andre's Capture Tree spooked Ichabod. He then heard the "plashy tramp of another traveler."

"Who are you?" he stammered, but received no reply. "Who are you?"

On mounting a rising ground—which brought the figure of his fellow traveler in relief against the sky, gigantic in height and muffled in a cloak—Ichabod was horror struck on perceiving that he was headless! But his horror increased on observing that the head rested on the pommel of his saddle.

A race against terror took off. "If I can just make it to that bridge!" thought the schoolmaster. "The headless horseman cannot cross!" Ichabod squeezed Gunpowder so hard he broke off the saddle and almost popped out the horse's one good eye. Ichabod reached the church bridge first. He turned to assure himself of the ghost's fiery disappearance. Alas! He caught the goblin in the very act of hurling his ghastly head. A shattering encounter with Crane's cranium ended the night's haunting.

The next morning, Hans van Ripper, Gunpowder's owner, found his horse grazing. But where was that scarecrow of a schoolmaster?

The schoolchildren had a holiday. The Dutch folk made a startling find beneath the bridge. There, scattered on the banks of the Pocantico, they

Ichabod beside the Headless Horseman, illustration. *By George Boughton for* Rip Van Winkle *and* The Legend of Sleepy Hollow *by Washington Irving*

spied the remains of their poor pedagogue. A hat, a piece of poetry to Katrina and, some cried, "Looky! 'Tis Crane's brains!" A few scoffed, "'Tis but pumpkin mash." No matter—Ichabod never again was seen in Sleepy Hollow.

Ah now, some claimed, "Crane had gone to the city and suffered a fate worse than being chased by a headless ghost; he had became a lawyer!" Brom, of course, married Katrina and always gave a knowing laugh whenever someone mentioned the pumpkin part of this tale.

The wise Dutch farm wives, who know these matters best, insist "the galloping Hessian spirited Ichabod to his grave that night." And in the cove where his old schoolhouse once stood, you still hear the ghostly singing of Ichabod Crane.

Chapter 1

BY THE NAME
WASHINGTON IRVING

On mounting a rising ground, which brought the figure of his fellow-traveller in relief against the sky, gigantic in height, and muffled in a cloak, Ichabod was horror-struck on perceiving that he was headless! But his horror was still more increased on observing that the head, which should have rested on his shoulders, was carried before him on the pommel of his saddle!....Now Ichabod cast a look behind to see if his pursuer should vanish, according to rule, in a flash of fire and brimstone. Just then he saw the goblin in his stirrups, in the very act of hurling his head at him. Ichabod endeavored to dodge the horrible missile, but it was too late.

—The Legend of Sleepy Hollow, *in Washington Irving's* The Sketch Book of Geoffrey Crayon, Gent. *6th ed. New York and London: C.S. Van Winkle and John Murray, 1820*

THE HORSEMAN'S APPEAL

Headless horsemen, from the Green Knight riding off head in hand after being decapitated by Sir Gawain to the wild skullduggery in Tim Burton's film *Sleepy Hollow*, have long thrilled us. Imbedded in our universal subconscious, he evokes primal fear and fascination. The favorite horseman is Washington Irving's "galloping Hessian of Sleepy Hollow."

The Legend of Sleepy Hollow was an instant hit when it first appeared in 1819. The Headless Horseman even makes a crowd-pleasing run at Disney's

Magic Kingdom. Recognized as the first major work by an American writer, *The Legend* is required reading at schools and universities. Everyone seems to both know and love the Headless Horseman of Sleepy Hollow.

In 1996, when General Motors closed down its North Tarrytown plant, the community looked for another way to bring in new business. Residents drew upon *The Legend*, renaming their hamlet Sleepy Hollow. A nearby village, once known as Dearman, had already taken the author's name, Irvington, in the nineteenth century.

Why do we love Irving's horseman? Russell Hubbard, a longtime historical interpreter at Washington Irving's homestead, Sunnyside, in Tarrytown, New York, gives a concise answer: "The scary chase appeals to our inner being. We all want a good fright!"

Irving taps into our inner Ichabod, dashing away from doom. He leaves with us the Headless Horseman ever riding as "the dominant spirit…that haunts this enchanted region" (*TLSH*, 5) of our imagination. We really want to know, where does he come from and why does he ride?

One definitive answer comes from "the most authentic historians of those parts" (*TLSH*, 5): Charlie Duda, another longtime Sunnyside interpreter and Hubbard's mentor. Charlie said he'd read everything on and by Irving. Speaking with an authoritative New York accent, he honed his knowledge on the subject of the Headless Horseman by addressing the public. When asked where Irving got *The Legend of Sleepy Hollow*, he would reply in characteristic form with the following bit of lore.

BELLS BECKON

One Sunday morning in 1818, when the fabled fog of the river Thames threatened to stop the day from breaking, two brothers hear the old bell of St. Martyr's Church tolling. The younger tarries, as the older presses on into the mist over London Bridge. He calls back, warning they'll be late for church.

The younger one is lost in the fog. He calls, telling his brother to look for a shape in the mist. The older one agrees to play along, saying, "All right! I see a horse and rider, only the rider needs a head!"

The younger one agrees and asks if it reminds him of the kind of stories they used to hear around the Hudson Valley. "Yes indeed, brother!" answers the elder. "What about the St. Martyr's bell tolling for us now? Let us go!"

Washington Irving, circa 1820, oil on canvas. *By Charles Robert Leslie, Historic Hudson Valley (ss.87.6 a-b).*

The younger, still studying those mists, replies, "Another bell calls for me. It rings, *Si Deus Pro Nobis, Quis Contra Nos* (If God is for us, who can be against us). Do you recall the church with that inscribed on it?"

"Of course! It's on the bell of Old Dutch Church of Sleepy Hollow! Washington! Are you homesick brother?"

"I'm reminded of a horseman who rode all along the Hudson. Forgive me brother, but I'm going to leave you to pray, while I go to write."

So the older one goes on to church, and the younger one goes on to write *The Legend of Sleepy Hollow*! Who were the brothers? Why, Peter and Washington Irving!

WASHINGTON IRVING

Pressing for proof of his account, Charlie followed Washington Irving's example, giving a delightfully indirect answer. *The Legend* came from a Dutch New Yorker, that old shabby gentleman who told it to Diedrich Knickerbocker, who left it in papers found by Geoffrey Crayon, the pseudonym used by Washington Irving. Charlie declared his account of Irving's inspiration for *The Legend* came from "all the biographers, who got their material from Irving's letters." Charlie Duda then interpreted the sources for us with the church bell story.

Distinguished biographers like Andrew Burstein and Stanley Williams generally agree with Charlie. Something in London's mists brought on homesickness and nostalgia for Sleepy Hollow, moving Irving to write *The Legend*. They go on to detail other sources Irving found inspiring in German and Scottish lore. Irving scholar Elisabeth Paling Funk postulates that Dutch American traditions shaped Irving's tale. Clearly the ride of the Headless Horseman began when something in the Sleepy Hollow air moved this New York City–raised author.

Born on April 4, 1783, during the British army occupation of Manhattan Island, Washington Irving came into the world just a couple weeks before General Washington assembled his troops on the Hudson to announce the formal end of the American War of Independence. The voices of Revolution—crying for liberty, calling for the pursuit of happiness—rang deep into the sensitive Washington Irving. A lifelong voracious reader, no doubt he read all he could on the struggle to create a new nation. Later he went on to write an exhaustive biography on his namesake, George Washington. An account given by his nursemaid, Lizzie, foreshadows the coming of America's first great writer.

A Bairn Named Washington

The Irving family's Scottish nursemaid spied the gentleman crossing Broadway from almost a block away. New York's wealthy merchants strove to stand out, garbed in gaudy colored frocks. George Washington, however, wore one of an understated elegant brown. A half a head above the street crowd, his calm, placid demeanor distinguished him further. He slipped into a shop. Lizzie took little Washington's hand and marched him straight in after the former general. The six-year-old tugged and tried to wiggle away. When he put his eyes upon the tall man, the little boy went still and solemn. Lizzie curtsied to the gentleman.

"Please pardon me your Excellency, but here's a bairn—was named after you."

The tall man looked upon the boy and gave a smile. Lizzie put her words into the boy's ear. "Washington, give a proper greeting, like you've been taught. Go on, say your name clear."

Little Washington Irving, awestruck, could not speak. The father of our country understood. Gently he placed his hand on the boy's head. The two smiled, perhaps giving each other blessings.

Lizzie, a good storyteller of a nursemaid, made sure the blessing became part of the Irving family lore. It shows a possible influence on young Washington, leading him to not only write about his namesake but to have an affinity for the history of American Revolution.

This incident would have occurred around the time of Washington's inauguration in New York City. Home to thirty-three thousand in 1790, Manhattan had long been the New World's most diverse city. The French Jesuit Isaac Jogues wrote in 1646: "On the island of Manhate, and in its environs, there may well be four or five hundred men of different sects and nations: the Director General told me that there were men of eighteen different languages."

Later, almost ninety years after the English transformed New Netherlands into New York, acclaimed Swedish traveler Pehr Kalm observed that the land between Manhattan and Albany was Dutch dominated. Dutch Reform churchgoers cried "nooit!" when their ministers started preaching in English in the early 1800s. Dutch ways endured late into the nineteenth century, with Presidents Theodore and Franklin Roosevelt reporting the use of Dutch phrases around their homes while growing up in the Hudson Valley.

Truly, Washington Irving, with a doting nursemaid, the pampered and protected youngest and eighth child of a Scot Presbyterian father and an

Episcopal mother, grew up in a diverse but Dutch world. Slipping off to explore the lower Hudson Valley, young Irving would sneak out for a night on the town after his father finished family prayers at nine. He'd meet up with his best comrades at Gouverneur Kemble's Cockloft Hall across the river in New Jersey. They called themselves the "Lads of Kilkenny." They gathered for evenings of revelry, pranks and satirical poem making. Young men with the names Brevoort, Kirke-Paulding and Swartout brought Dutch ways and words to Washington Irving.

TIPPING LEATHERHEADS

Irving, in *The Legend*, carefully crafts a rival to chase Ichabod away from the bounteous beautiful Katrina van Tassel. The double-jointed Abraham van Brunt was known as Brom Bones and famed for his pranks. Apparently, Brom's best work took form when he disguised himself as the galloping ghost to drive and even drag off the interloping schoolmaster.

Those Lads of Kilkenny practiced an early version of this prank on the poor night watchmen of late eighteenth-century New York. Working at night as a guard at various corners in New York City had its benefits. A man could labor by day in a shop, at a trade or on the waterfront; by night he could get paid to don a watchman's leather cap and settle into the narrow little guard booth. There was just enough room to lean and doze. If luck kept crime away, the watchman only had to wake up to shout out the hour and that all is well. You'd collect a pretty penny in pay for all your slumbers.

What could make for a better target for the Lads of Kilkenny? One night, after family prayers, Washington slinked out his window under the gable. Dashing by the Dutch Church toward John Street, he met up with his fellow Lads. What did Lady Fortune drop in their laps? A leatherhead was already nodding off on his watch! The Lads lifted a rope from a horse post. They secured it around the sleepy sentry's booth. Letting forth a conquering hoot, they yanked, toppling the little guard's station.

Clattering over the cobblestone street, the Lads dragged the Old Charlie, his howling protests fueling their spirited laughter. When they'd had enough of their prank and came into view of another watchman, they dropped the rope, turned a corner and caught their breath after the sidesplitting fun. They, like Brom Bones at the end of *The Legend*, "gave a hearty laugh" (*TLSH*, 72) when hearing about their prank.

Road to Sleepy Hollow, 2008. *Photo by Todd Atteberry, www.thehistorytrekker.com.*

RAMBLES AND READINGS, CUSTOMS AND HEARTACHE

When in his teens, Washington also traveled on a sloop with a Dutch-speaking skipper and an African American crew. Irving's first excursions into the Hudson Highlands cast a spell. He wrote, "What a time of intense delight was that first sail through the Highlands. How solemn and thrilling the scene as we anchored at night at the foot of those mountains, clothed with overhanging forests; and every thing grew dark and mysterious."

There young Irving hunted for squirrels but found folklore. He drank in the local tales, landscapes and characters. Gathering stories from Dutch farm wives, Irish laborers and a knowing "African sage," he later bundled them all into his fabulous storyteller, Diedrich Knickerbocker. This venerable pipe-smoking, wine-swilling itinerant bard spun yarns of river spirits, forlorn witches, wailing ghosts and the galloping Hessian to Irving's equally fictitious but just as distinguished "sketch" writer, Geoffrey Crayon, gentleman. *The Legend of Sleepy Hollow*, however, along with his other famed work, *Rip Van Winkle*, took root in German lore.

Always an avid reader, Irving devoured the German folk and fairy tales collected in the early 1800s by the Brothers Grimm and Johann Otmar. He turned the tale of *Peter Klaus the Goatherd* into *Rip Van Winkle*. Gottfried Augustus Burger's epic poem, *Der Wilde Jager*, also based in German lore, and the *Wild Huntsmen*, the version written by Irving's friend Sir Walter Scott, formed Irving's Headless Horseman.

Irving carefully crafted together story elements from diverse sources. He wove German folklore into his own experiences of the Dutch on the Hudson. He also borrowed a few ghostly plot devices from Robert Burns's *Tam O'Shanter*. Further, while living in Great Britain, his nostalgia fueled his desire to write about home. Add Irving's own melancholia over love and death to his uniquely American characters, and the "galloping Hessian" began his Sleepy Hollow run from his head to paper in 1818.

Lady Fortune tormented Washington Irving before granting success to his *Sketch Book*. Studying law under the esteemed Ogden Hoffman, Washington Irving found "an insuperable repugnance" for his chosen profession. Why practice the law when he had become the talk of the town writing humorous sendups of "Yorkers" in his magazine *Salmagundi*? Then, just as his writing led to a triumph in 1809 with the publication of *Diedrich Knickerbocker's History of New-York*, his satire of Dutch colonial days, death came calling: his sister, Nancy, and father, William, passed away within a few months of each other.

The Grim Reaper was just beginning to cast his shadow over the promising young author. He noted how a young lady, "timid, shy, silent," swept up his heart. Matilda Hoffman, his boss's daughter, was in her early teens when she first sparked Irving's interest while he tutored her in drawing and poetry. She showed, Irving wrote in a letter, "mantling modesty," which was beginning to peel away, revealing something sublime.

By the Name Washington Irving

When *A History* started selling, Matilda fell ill with "consumption," otherwise known as tuberculosis. Washington served as her enduring nurse. She "grew beautiful and more angelical" as the disease progressed, he tenderly declared. She died just before her eighteenth birthday.

Matilda never left Washington's heart. He cherished her Bible, prayer book and memory as lifelong keepsakes. The theme of unattainable love occurs in *The Legend of Sleepy Hollow*, with Ichabod Crane longing for Katrina van Tassel and "her vast expectations" (*TLSH*, 6).

Critics, like biographer Stanley L. Williams, blame Washington's lifelong bachelorhood on his lost love, Matilda. Granted, years later, the thirty-seven-year-old author fell for another fay teenage girl, Miss Emily Foster. He placed all the girls he loved on an angelic pedestal. Thus, like Ichabod, Irving never found true love. Washington, however, knew better than to fall for a feisty "coquette" like Katrina van Tassel.

People often point to the tombstone of Catriena Ecker van Tassel, at the Old Dutch Church, and proclaim, "That's the young woman in *The Legend of Sleepy Hollow*!" America's first author found his Katrina not in a graveyard but among the independent, free-thinking Dutch American lasses he met up and down the Hudson. The steadfast and wily ways of Irving's other Dutch characters, Brom Bones and Baltus van Tassel, introduced the world to genuine Americans. Bold, brash Brom looks especially like an American archetype. Still, when Irving sets up Brom in the guise of a ghost to ward off an unwanted suitor, he's following an old Dutch custom. Plus Ichabod suffers a fate worse than being chased from marriage by a headless ghost when "partly in mortification…he turned politician…and had been made a justice in the ten pound court!" (*TLSH*, 72). The humor riding just below the surface in *The Legend* here spills over.

Clearly, there's more to Irving's horseman than a love lost and a ghostly gallop. It's not a mere knockoff of a German fairy tale, sprinkled with Dutch customs. Certainly, Stanley Williams, in the 1930s, scoffed at Irving's *Sketch Book* stories as "pilferings" from "age-old legends." Andrew Burstein, in his 2007 biography, however, proves "Washington Irving looms large." He brought "important changes to culture." Rip Van Winkle, the Headless Horseman, Katrina, Brom Bones and Ichabod Crane are all the first folk characters in American literature. Washington Irving's classics are, indeed, wordy, romantic and sentimental. Nevertheless, they have what interpreter Russell Hubbard described as "enduring appeal."

The *Little Man in Black*, an Old Wolf and Heath

Our author also got a little help losing a head from a *Little Man in Black*. Aaron Burr, lightly disguised as the title character in this Irving tale, is described as wearing a "halo of genius." Longtime friends, the Irving family stood by the little man even after his infamous duel with Alexander Hamilton. Irving, in his tale, praised Burr's legal mind. The man also had a head for story details. Dining with the vice president turned villain just before his first trip to Europe in 1804, the young lawyer turned writer gleaned an unusual war anecdote.

A distinguished officer during the American Revolution, Burr served as an aide to General Israel "Wolf" Putnam. The old soldier was himself legendary. He earned this nickname at age twenty after slaying a wolf barehanded. A British officer in the French and Indian War, Putnam escaped Huron warriors trying to burn him at the stake. Later when British dragoons raced to nab "Old Put," the rebel general escaped by riding his horse down a stone footpath in Horseneck (Greenwich), Connecticut. Frightened militiamen at the Battle of Bunker Hill said it was Putnam who steadied them while the Redcoats approached. He supposedly warned, "Don't fire till you see the whites of their eyes!"

General Putnam hanged several spies—one until he was "dead, dead, dead!" He also saw soldiers get their heads blown off; one of them was Abraham Onderdonck. He was "killed by a cannon ball from the enemy, separating his head from his shoulders." Did Irving and Burr chat about decapitation over their lunch? Certainly, the tale-loving Irving pumped his battle-scarred companion for old Revolutionary War stories. Biographer Burstein states, "So, it is not unreasonable to consider that Irving might have known the details of this (headless) story."

Irving, a voracious reader and dedicated listener, certainly knew detailed stories from the Battle of White Plains. Thousands of British forces, with regulars, Loyalists and, of course, their Hessian henchmen, marched to a misty marsh the Native folk called Quarropas to chase American Continentals and Minutemen off Chatterton's Hill. Close to Halloween 1776, Hessians commanded by the fierce Colonels Rall, Heister and Donop spearheaded the British assault. The unseasoned American troops under Washington, Putnam, Heath and Lee fought hard for a time. Lacking cannon, save for a few captained by Alexander Hamilton, the rebels fell back and endured to fight another day.

One curious entry in the journal of General William Heath appears to be the holy grail for the source of the Headless Horseman. Heath wrote of witnessing a Hessian artilleryman lose his head at the Battle of White Plains on October 31, 1776!

HEAD IN THE MUD HESSIAN

Private Joseph Plumb Martin, who also fought under Old Put, set down in his thoroughly engaging journal a couple of touching tales concerning German soldiers. Returning after a year or so on the scene of the Battle of White Plains, Martin's unit encountered Hessian remains. Decaying bones and separated skulls had been left out in the open. He mourns the "poor Hessian dying in a fight for a foreign land only to be left unburied." Further, the compassionate private recounts an event truly worthy of Washington Irving:

The Van Tassel house, Tarrytown, New York. *Photo by Louis Glaser's Process, published by* Harper's Monthly, *April 1876. From the collection of the Highland Studio, Inc., Cold Spring, NY.*

> *There was an Irishman belonging to our infantry, who after the affray was over, seeing a wounded man belonging to the enemy lying in the road and being unable to help himself, took pity on him, as he was in danger of being trodden upon by the horses, and having shouldered him was staggering off with his load, in order to get him to a place of more safety. While crossing a worn out bridge over a very muddy brook, he happened to jostle the poor fellow more than usual, who cried out.*
>
> *"Good rebel, don't hurt poor Hushman."*
>
> *"Who you call a rebel, you scoundrel?" said the Irishman, and tossed him off his shoulders as unceremoniously as though he had been a log of wood. He fell with his head in the mud, and as I passed I saw him struggling for life, but I had other business on my hands than to stop to assist him. I did sincerely pity the poor mortal…Most likely there he made his final exit.*

Stories like these circulated in New York after independence. It's easy to imagine how accounts of Hessians, heads lost in the mud, their skulls lying on the ground, could find their way to Washington Irving. Indeed, these tales do appear in *The Legend*. Brom Bones sets the scene for his anecdote of a "race with the galloping Hessian" by first egging on Sleepy Hollow's veterans to tell their old war stories. Irving gives us a hint on how he works with his narrators' little preface to those battle tales: "Just sufficient time had elapsed to enable each storyteller to dress up his tale with a little becoming fiction, and, in the indistinctness of his recollection, to make himself the hero of every exploit" (*TLSH*, 50).

Irving harvested these recollections from former fighters like Joseph Plumb Martin, Aaron Burr and Generals Putnam and Heath. He "dressed them up" with German lore, Dutch customs, his own heartache and dead-on accurate sketches of local characters encountered. Then through the marshy mists and haze of battle, a galloping horseman rattles all to the core. The rider's head is lodged in the crook of his sword arm! Truly, this is a tale worth finding, exploring and developing.

TARRYTOWN TAVERN TALES

Van Tassel's tavern, situated on a rise above Tarrytown on Hudson, once welcomed all along Albany Post Road. When two New York City lads, Washington Irving and his buddy James Kirke-Pauling, dropped in for grog and grub, they'd encounter the local denizens: Westchester farmers waiting for the mill to grind for their "tarwe" or Dutch wheat, travelers aching from a bone-jangling carriage, idle tradesmen and grizzled veterans from the Revolution.

One blue-bearded Dutchman brags about the small cannon he fired at a British warship marauding on the Hudson. He tells them, "I would have sunk the vessel had not me cannon blowed up!"

The young men laugh. A well-to-do merchant, once a mounted officer, describes parrying a bullet away from General Washington. Again they chuckle. So the locals bring out their sure-fire yarn. Speaking in hushed tones they describe a ghastly scene:

> *We fought at White Plains under MacDougal! The Hessians attacked us on Chatterton's Hill. Some stood seven feet tall, with two rows of teeth! They came after us, but we held them till an English cannon ball tore open a Massachusetts' man's leg. Those New Englanders ran. They feared the same would happen to them if they stayed. We feared them Hessians! They shot three of our men that they'd captured. Hessians grant no quarter. Had we not run too, we'd not be here to tell you the tale.*

They whispered about witnessing men get their heads blown off in battle too. Perhaps young Irving bought the veterans a round for the storytelling.

Years later, threads of these yarns certainly appear in *The Legend* and other Irving works. He may have met in Van Tassel's a couple of other interesting characters: a local trapper, part Indian, who acted as Irving's guide, and a charming coquette of a wench with the common Dutch name of Catrina.

A LOVE FOR ALL THINGS REVOLUTIONARY AND DUTCH

The watchman-dragging, Hudson-wandering, lore and language–loving Washington Irving found plenty of inspiration along the ancient Mahicanituck or old North River. Doubtless the land and people on the Hudson infused him with a love of this country. The land then was wild, ragged and raw. The only people who really knew its stories were the Natives, the Dutch and their slaves. Irving knew they were disappearing into the great waves of change and immigration.

The American Revolution must have been especially intriguing to a young man named after the cause's greatest hero. Family friend Aaron Burr filled young Irving's head with war exploits, as did all those tavern tales gleaned from the old Minutemen. It's possible, then, that Irving read or at least knew the memoirs of Joseph Plumb Martin and William Heath.

Growing up with the waning of Dutch voices and customs, Irving captured a sense of the 1640s' New Netherlands in his wildly popular book *Diedrich Knickerbocker's History of New-York*. Later, seeking to perpetuate endearing Dutch customs like visitations from "Sinter Klaas," Irving helped transform a dour bishop into jolly old Santa Claus. Scholars, like Elisabeth Paling Funk, contend Irving spoke some Dutch. Surely, Dutch New York customs, pranks and all, would interest and inspire Washington Irving.

This stirred up the writer's passion. Again, add love lost, a long time away from home and a fascination with fairy tales, and when a bell tolled over the Thames, Irving heard it ring in Sleepy Hollow. Now we turn to the stories, the lore and some history surrounding Washington Irving and the Headless Horseman.

Chapter 2

"THE PLACE WAS BEWITCHED"

An old Indian chief, the prophet of wizard of his tribe, held his pow-wows there before the country was discovered by Master Hendrick Hudson. Certain it is, the place still continues under the sway of some witching power, that holds a spell over the minds of the good people, causing them to walk in a continual sense of reverie.

They are given to all kinds of marvelous beliefs; are subject to trances and visions, and frequently see strange sights and hear music and voices in the air. The whole neighborhood abounds with local tales, haunted spots and twilight superstitions (TLSH, 4).

A sensation of spirits pervades Sleepy Hollow and the surrounding lower Hudson Valley. This unique haunted history ranges from Manhattan's northernmost point where the "spitting devil" hides. The haunting infiltrates the dense suburbs overlying the ancient Dutch farmlands in Rockland County, home to the last witch trial in New York. It pervades the enchanted waters of the Tappan Zee and finally reaches into the shadows of the Hudson Highlands.

Judith Richardson, in her scholarly book *Possessions: The History and Uses of Haunting in the Hudson Valley*, states:

> There are ghost of Indians and Dutchmen, and of Revolutionary War soldiers and spies, ghosts of presidents, slaves, priests, and laborers. There are neighborhoods of ghost and family ghosts, and ghosts whose identities

are unknown. There are haunted cemeteries, houses, mountains, bridges, and factories. There are Spook Rocks and Spook Hollows, and Spook Fields. There are places haunted by famous ghosts.

Richardson goes on to put forth this hypothesis: "Ghosts operate as a particular, and peculiar, kind of social memory, an alternate form of history-making in which things forgotten, discarded, or repressed become foregrounded."

Bewitchment here occurs within all the layers of people who came and settled the region. If the newcomers forget they are in Sleepy Hollow country, a ghost pops up to remind them. This is exactly what happens when the Connecticut Yankee, Ichabod Crane, arrives in Dutch Sleepy Hollow to teach. Thrilled by the spooky locale, the schoolmaster remained blithely oblivious to the local Dutch American customs. Thus he eventually receives a lesson from the Headless Horseman!

Washington Irving, near the opening of his *Legend*, explains what happens when people enter these environs: "However wide awake they may have been before they entered that sleepy region, they are sure, in a little time, to inhale the witching influence of the air, and begin to grow imaginative, to dream dreams, and see apparitions" (*TLSH*, 4).

This witching influence began with the first "layer" of people. The native Lenape, Weckquasgeek, Wappinger, Siwanoy, Munsee and Mahican of the Mahicanituck (the Hudson River) open the door to the haunting yet to come. The Legend of Mahicanituck and Pocantico stems from a mythic meeting of two rivers at the heart of the region.

THE LEGEND OF MAHICANITUCK AND POCANTICO

Our grandmothers tell those of us who listen of love found and lost by the Mahicanituck. When the Grandfathers, the Delaware people, neglected to say "En-na-shee"—thank you to the sleeping giant—he stood up. The lake, which his great body dammed, rushed beneath his legs, pushing into the ocean. The great waters pushed back, forming Mahicanituck, "the river-that-flows-both-ways."

Twirling over the Hokohonkgus, the place where the waters fall and twist with eels, a deep pool formed at Mahicanituck's side. Leaping into the mist, dashing over the stones to escape into her hollow, Pocantico danced her kent-kow alone. Always moving himself, Mahicanituck never tarried long enough to dance with her.

Then the Thunder Beings fought. Standing as tall as trees with bodies like birds and heads like men, they raged. Flapping their monstrous wings, the old ones bellowed; the young ones crackled sharply back. Their battle drove Mahicanituck hard and very high. The Mahicanituck swelled over the hollow, into Pocantico. He swirled in with her.

"Hi-yee!" he shrieked. "We two rivers move as one!" Together they danced into a kent-kow.

The Thunder Beings soon abandoned their fight. Drawing back wind and water, they pulled Mahicanituck apart from Pocantico. They left the place of Hokohonkgus, flattened and writhing with eels. Where the two rivers had danced, an immense chestnut tree grew. The Mahican people held powwows, dancing kent-kows beneath the great branches.

Now, that tree has fallen, and those who once lived near it have mostly gone away. Still, when the Thunder Beings make a great storm, Mahicanituck returns to Pocantico. They again dance their kent-kow at the waterfall.

This story emerges from the Algonquin words Mahicanituck and Pocantico. Mahicanituck essentially means "the river that flows both ways." Earlier creation myths suggest the awakening of a sleeping giant. A lake, which formed against his body, races to the sea, becoming that ever-shifting river. Coincidentally, this tale echoes the scientific explanation of the Hudson River's formation. When the last Ice Age ended some twenty thousand years ago, lingering glaciers in the region broke like old dams. Pent-up waters, known as Lake Albany, flowed again into an ancient riverbed. They gouged a deep channel reaching miles into the ocean. Eventually, the meltwater subsided, and the Atlantic pushed back. The Hudson River then returned but now as an arm of the sea, a tidal estuary, rising high and north and south all the way to Troy, New York.

The Pocantico River now flows through Sleepy Hollow hard by the Old Dutch Church. It cascades pastorally over the Philipseburg Manor milldam to meander into the Hudson. When, in 1681, the superintendent of Frederick Philipse's manor first wrote down on his lordship's deed "pocantico," a Native phrase for "a stream between the two hills," he identified a local feature for his boss. There a small waterfall broke up the Pocantico River just before it reached the Hudson River. An immense chestnut tree, later known as the Hokohonkgus, stood nearby.

"Pak," in the Munsee Algonquin tongue, roughly refers to a flat place. "Kent-kow" tripped off the tongues of Dutch and English settlers as

Spook hand on Ichabod, 1899 illustration. *By Frederich Simpson Coburn for* The Legend of Sleepy Hollow *by Washington Irving.*

"canticoy," now an archaic word signifying a dance. Local Native peoples evidently met under the Hokohonkgus tree to hold high councils. The landmark tree, which stood until 1905, certainly caught the attention of Washington Irving. Local Indian lore would captivate curious young Irving, especially stories of the land being bewitched.

When those two rivers meet, watch out for a stormy dance! Once every hundred years or so, the Thunder Beings reunite the Hudson with the Pocantico. Hurricane Floyd arranged for another such engagement in 2003. Situated adjacent to the dam, Sleepy Hollow's Philipseburg Manor came very close to being washed out. Then site manager Melinda Terpening just barely saved the historic Hudson Valley site from destruction by organizing a sandbag brigade against the surging merging waters. It seems where these two rivers converge the spell of a "kent-kow" will pervade. The curse of Mahicanituck and Pocantico's dance still falls on Sleepy Hollow.

SPOOKED STONES

Another local legend offers another explanation for the spooky sensation hanging over this region. Dutch settlers, eager to plant their "tarwe" or wheat, found an open field beside a great stone. Inauspiciously, it turned out to be a burial ground from which the Native locals warned the Dutch to keep away with their iron plows. They told their new neighbors the grounds were tainted by a spell.

A local Weckquasgeek chief once called a war council on that great stone near the great chestnut tree. He condemned an interloping tribe: "They have come here where we live, to take game, pick berries and eat shellfish. Yet, they offer us no wampum belts, not even a pinch of tobacco in gratitude! They give us only threats of war. We cannot share lands by the Pocantico, with these disrespectful people!" The talking stick in hand strengthened his words. When the chief demanded, "What warrior will join me in fighting them?" no one replied. They feared the powerful enemy.

At last, the silence was broken by the creak of old bones. A sage known for dreaming true dreams took up the talking stick: "We must place upon the ones who will not make peace, a deep spell."

The tribal council agreed. The wise one told them to gather the necessary plants. They danced and chanted to conjure a curse. The invaders fell into a deathly sleep. Nature turned them into bones, their skulls stones beneath soil.

The Dutch farmers dismissed the Native tale as superstition. They went ahead, turning over the cursed stones with their metal plows. Disturbed, the captive spirits groaned in agony but escaped into the ethers of the Hollow. This caused the Dutch to fall "under the sway of some witching power, that holds a spell over the minds of the good people, causing them to walk in a continual reverie" (*TLSH*, 4).

Washington Irving walked in a kind of reverie as a "stripling" lad. Certainly, like those good Dutch people, he fell under the sway of bewitching stories. We see this sense for the Dutch under a spell in his writing. They became the jocular caricatures we love. Renowned twentieth-century river writer Carl Carmer noted, in his 1939 book, *The Hudson*, that Washington Irving "amusingly" depicted New Netherlanders as "wide-rear, slow-wit Dutch fatheads." Carmer goes on describe the Dutch settlers as "hard blond traders," exactly the kind of folk ready to scoff at an Indian burial ground. He goes on to put forth a picture of the Dutch as contentious, feisty people. "These men and woman were actually quick to anger, peppery, captious, nervously active." Irving's illustrations of the Dutch show more affection. Here's how he paints a scene of the New Netherlanders mustering for a war against the Swedish colony to the south in his 1809 book, *Diedrich Knickerbocker's History of New-York*:

> *First came the Van Bummels…these were short fat men, wearing exceedingly large trunk-breeches, renowned for their feats of the trencher… Then Couenhovens of Sleepy Hollow; these gave rise to a jolly race of publicans, who first discovered the magic artifice of conjuring a quart of wine into a pint bottle…lastly came the Knickerbockers of the great town of Scaghtikoke, where the folk lay stones upon the houses in windy weather, lest they should be blown away.*

Ten years later, in *The Legend of Sleepy Hollow*, these same charming contrary folk are ready for a ride by a Headless Horseman. A portrait then emerges from these two authors of Dutch Americans as people excitable enough to believe in spirits. Further, they will take action on omens.

One story reflects this Dutch colonial spirit in Sleepy Hollow. Frederick Philipse arrived in the New Netherlands with next to nothing and wound up creating the richest family in the colonies.

CUFFEY'S PROPHECY

Frederick Philipse was blessed with ways to see things through to a profit. He arrived around 1640 in the New Netherlands colonial town of New Amsterdam. Lacking money, he believed his God-given noble blood would bring him wealth. Taking work in the growing colony as a carpenter, he soon found it more profitable to sell rather than hammer nails. Young Philipse put this money into a tavern and managed to marry a wealthy widow. Soon he became the lord of thousands of acres of "hunting-grounds from Spuyten Duvyil to Croton on Hudson." There he determined to turn his wilderness into a proper productive manor and farm.

Philipse's wife, Margaret Hardenbroeck, got rich in the slave trade. Seeing how skillfully the Africans worked, Philipse shrewdly sent them to expand his country house in "Slaper's Haven," Dutch for sleeper's port, the secondary harbor in the region after Tarrytown.

Settlers renting farms from Philipse had grain to grind. This blessing Philipse acknowledged in two ways: he began to build a mill and a church. Working on the church, he gazed down the Pocantico where his mill would stand; Frederick noticed grain piling up. Finding no blessing without profit, he directed his head slave, Cuffey, to stop work on the church, dam up the river and finish the mill.

Cuffey respectfully submitted. "God, sir, should come before grain." The lord of the manor respectfully disagreed. This did not sit well with the slave. Sleeping in that spellbound hollow, a nightmare visited Cuffey: a terrible storm would roar up the river and wash away the dam unless the church was completed first! The dutiful servant reported his dream to the master. Philipse scoffed at his superstitious slave.

The next night, the dream returned. The slave gave warning, but the landlord again ignored him. On the third night, the storm really came. Raging, it ripped down the works of men, letting the Pocantico dance into the Mahicanituck near the Hokohonkgus. Cuffey then had a different dream. He told Philipse no dam would ever hold until the church was built.

Humbled, the nervous Dutch lord took heed of the African's intuition. He ordered his men to first complete the church. And the lord of Philipseburg Manor himself took up his old hammer and built the pulpit.

Cuffey seems to have fallen under the spell released when Dutch farmers turned over stony Native graves. He walked with "a sense of reverie." He dreamed a prophetic dream. Around the church the seer-slave saw built, there's risen the dam, roads, culverts, farms, factories, suburban houses and cell towers. Though redirected, the Pocantico spirits out from under those layers of change. The Native American appears like a fleeting shadow in the forest in *The Legend of Sleepy Hollow*. Yet the influence of local Native people, filtered deeply into Irving's classic, still holds sway over the entire region.

HOKOHONKGUS TREE

The etymology of Hokohonkgus suggests a small waterfall associated with eels at a small hill, but it is the tree that holds sway over Sleepy Hollow. Trees are a power presence in *The Legend* and in the Hudson Valley. They not only shape the landscape but also draw in sensations of both sweetness and scariness. Snow covered and shaking, they appear as ghostlike entities to Ichabod Crane. The site (and sight) of the monstrous tulip tree, where the "unfortunate Major Andre" was caught in 1780, initiates the frightful journey of the schoolmaster. The grand Hokohonkgus reigned over all in the area until a storm brought it down in 1905. Today its pervasive ways reemerge from the layers of farms and suburbs. Westchester, even with almost one million people, is almost as wooded as it was in colonial days. An immense tulip tree again marks the spot where American Revolutionary "skinners" captured Andre. Rows of poplar trees, patched with skin-toned bark, stand as guardians of Sleepy Hollow cemetery today.

MORE SPOOKED STONES

An old colonial rule of thumb contended it took one man one year to clear one acre of land. The New Netherlands in the lower Hudson Valley, in spite of the dense trees and the groaning stones, proved most fertile. Westchester in the 1700s became the breadbasket for the colonies. Dutch, then English, plows would inevitably unearth Native spells and buried bones. More stories rose from the rocks around Sleepy Hollow.

Spook or Council Rock, near Gory Brook Road, is the site of the Weckquasgeek sleeping spell. Some Native people along the Mahicanituck jokingly referred to grave sites as "pumpkin patches." Several other scary stones mark the Sleepy Hollow landscape. Tales abound at Spook, Balance, Widow and especially Raven Rock.

Spirits of Sleepy Hollow, 1893 illustration. *By George Boughton for* Rip Van Winkle *and* The Legend of Sleepy Hollow *by Washington Irving*

Again, Spook Rock was the spot where the Weckquasgeek council cast the sleeping spell. Balance Rock, once near Tarrytown Lakes, fell when a medicine man accidentally fired a gun. The Thunder Beings cursed him with a jolt of lightning, leaving a print visible in the tumbled stone today. Widow Rock harbors a forlorn form wailing for her dead husband. She may be another twist on the White Lady of Raven Rock. This woeful woman offers a few stories, but she always moans before storms. The White Lady is the most frequently encountered ghost reported in Sleepy Hollow.

Distinguished folklorist Edgar M. Bacon places the Legend of the Star Maiden at Spook Rock, Sleepy Hollow. Others declare this story originates with the Iroquois, northern non-Algonquin speaking peoples. The many versions of this legend from Japan to Greece show a universal theme of love and loss to a star spirit. The Star Maiden tale also echoes elements found in *The Legend of Sleepy Hollow*.

Legend of the Star Maiden

One night, a dozen dancing star-eyed sky maidens enchant a young brave returning from a deer hunt. He abandons the kill he was bringing back to his family to pounce like a panther upon the youngest star maiden. Against advice from the wise women, he makes the ethereal lass his wife. They soon have a starry child.

Later the star-sisters return to Sleepy Hollow. They scoop up their earthbound youngest for another sky dance. Thinking the dance just lasted for the night, the star-bride returns for her husband and child. She finds three years have passed. Motherless, the baby refused to eat and died. Her forlorn husband wandered off, never to be seen again.

Grief stricken, the star-wife transforms into a will-o'-the-wisp, an earthbound spirit of lights. Flickering, she seeks her husband around Spook Rock in Sleepy Hollow. The remaining star-sisters still dance in the night sky as the tiny constellation known as the Pleiades: "The fireflies, too, which sparkled most vividly in the darkest places, now and then startled him, as one of uncommon brightness would stream across his path" (*TLSH*, 12).

Chapter 3

TALES OF THE TAPPAN ZEE

*In the bosom of one of those spacious coves which indent the eastern shore of the Hudson, at that broad expansion of the river denominated by the ancient Dutch navigators the Tappan Zee…they always prudently shortened sail and implored the protection of St. Nicholas when they crossed (*TLSH, *1).*

A three-mile-wide expanse in the Hudson River provides a gateway to the lore of the lower Hudson Valley. This sea sets the stage for the ghosts of Sleepy Hollow. It gives the Headless Horseman his mystifying backdrop. "Tappan Zee" is a unique partnering of an Algonquin and a Dutch word. "Tuppane" refers to the cold waters under the shadows of west bank cliffs called the Palisades. "Zee" is an archaic Dutch word for a small sea. The name brings two differing peoples together in one place. Various stories from that reach of the river reflect a clash of cultures. It foretells the surprise and mystery found in *The Legend of Sleepy Hollow*. Tales of the Tappan Zee often mix opposing forces, like mist and mountain, wind and tide, to create drama on the Hudson.

HENRY HUDSON AND THE SEVERED HAND

When Henry Hudson sailed the *Half Moon* up a sprawling waterway he dubbed "the river of mountains," he made several discoveries. First, this wide tidal river was not the Northwest Passage to the riches of Cathay that

Mahicans greeting Henry Hudson, 1876. Wood print. *Published by* Harper's Monthly, *April 1876. From the collection of the Highland Studio, Inc., Cold Spring, N.Y.*

Hudson had been hired to route out by the Dutch East India Company. Second, the region looked bountiful. His mate and journalist, Robert Juet, scribed, "This is a very good Land to fall with, and a pleasant Land to see." Further, Juet found "this River is full of fish." Hudson and his crew of about twenty English and Dutch sailors expressed ambivalence about the indigenous people. Juet wrote, "The people of the Countrey came aboord us, making shew of love, gave us tabacco and Indian Wheat...but we durst not trust them." He often repeated that refrain.

The people of that country—the Lenape, Raritan, Canarsie, Wappingers, Weckquasgeek, Esopus, Munsee and, of course, the Mahican—also perceived those who crossed the great salty waters with fearsome awe. The progress of what appeared to be a great canoe pulled by clouds drew curious Weckquasgeek people from their village, Wysquaqua, down to the banks of the Mahicanituck. Gazing out from what is now Dobbs Ferry (several miles south of Sleepy Hollow), they wondered if the hairy faces and pale skin meant they looked upon animals, sick men or spirits. Undaunted, they sensed an opportunity for trade.

Launching several canoes, they chanted a welcome and offered shellfish, deer meat, berries and beaver skins. They swapped with Hudson's sailors for buttons, cloth, beads, knives and pots made of miraculously strong metals. Again Juet glowered, "We darest not trust them." Apparently the ship's mate wrote prophetically: Hudson ordered John Colman and a handful of men into the shallop boat to explore Newark Bay. They found a land "pleasant with Grasse and Flowers, and goodly Trees." Unfortunately, a misunderstanding with the Raritan tribe left Colman dead with an arrow through the throat. The European explorers took two Native men from a trading party as captives to ensure they'd not be attacked again. Later, the pair surprised the crew by jumping into the river, swimming to shore and taunting back at the *Half Moon* in "scorne."

Juet, however, reports in his very next sentence, "There wee found very loving people." Farther upriver, near present-day Kingston, they enjoyed the hospitality of the Esopus Indians. Sharing a pipe of fine tobacco, the Native hosts served the ravenous Europeans wild pigeon and roasted dog. Hudson and Juet accepted gifts of pemmican venison. Shallow waters forced the *Half Moon* to turn back near Waterford, New York. The only riches they'd find would come from the lands Hudson claimed for the Netherlands.

Returning through the Hudson Highlands under the shadow of Donder-Berg, on the Tappan Zee, a gang of Munsee saw a chance to get at some riches for themselves. Sneaking up in a canoe, they boarded the *Half Moon* and swiped some of Juet's red bandoliers and other sundries. Hudson's master mate shot one of the thieves. Launching their shallop, the ship's cook and a few other sailors began hotly pursuing the canoe. One Munsee slipped underwater. Grabbing the small Dutch boat at the bow, he tried flipping it over. Enraged, the "Cooke" drew his sword and sliced off the poor fellow's hand. He sank under the ever-shifting Mahicanituck. The others dove out of the canoe and swam to shore. Juet got back his possessions at a deadly price.

Word spread of the dangerous ways of these strangers-who-cross-the-salty-waters-with-skin-like-snow-and-hair-on-their-faces-like-animals. Soon, the *Half Moon* found fierce Sint Sick warriors from Senasqua (Croton Point) and Weckquasgeek from Wysquaqua paddling toward them. Hudson and Juet ordered their "falcon," or cannon, fired. They added a few rounds of musketry. The Europeans reported about a half-dozen "Savages" killed. Native accounts, however, told of over three times as many deaths, resulting from the strangers' fire sticks.

The Donder-Berg, illustration. *Published by* Harper's Monthly, *April 1876. From the collection of the Highland Studio, Inc., Cold Spring, NY.*

Surely, this strange tale of trade and death merited a retelling under the Hokohonkgus tree. Twenty years later, when Dutch settlers began arriving in the Hudson Valley, they heard stories of the 1609 encounter. When the Native peoples spoke of Europeans, they also had reason to end their story with "we darest not trust them!" Perhaps the memorable first encounter between European and Native American cultures along the Hudson River prompted the chieftain's spell that Washington Irving mentions at the beginning of his *Legend*.

IMPS!

The deadly 1609 encounters along the Tappan Zee yielded eerie feelings about the cliffs and high hills bounding the region. Relentless tides, erratic winds and the foggy Highlands moved people, both Native and European, to sense something more than nature at work on that part of the river.

When rogue waves swamped canoes and surprise storms sank sloops, people determined this was the supernatural at play. The Natives referred to river spirits as a kind of "Manitou." Dutch sailors found a danger zone ranging from around Croton Point and Haverstraw Bay to the "worregat" or wind gate between Storm King Mountain and Breakneck Ridge in the Highlands above West Point. Who made the Protestant Dutch skippers on the Hudson hark back to a medieval Catholic practice of praying to Saint Nicholas for protection? 'Twas Dwerg, the "Heer of the Donder-Berg," culprit imp of the Hudson River Highlands!

Long before the times of tractor-trailers, trains and steamships, sloops hauled on the Hudson. The great river's whims required a sturdy Dutch-designed craft with a fixed bowsprit, a moveable keel board and three sails. The top one, the "skyscraper," resembled a colonial tricorn cap. The sloop could deliver passengers and goods from New York to Albany, sometimes in just forty-eight hours. No ship, however, by any power entirely rules the river. Dutch sailors knew where to shorten sail and when to pray.

Sailors on the Hudson spoke the language of the river—Dutch—well into the 1800s. They took on runaway servants and slaves who found freedom by learning every cove and channel on the Hudson. Sloop skippers navigated to Albany by a series of fourteen reaches. Each one presented unique challenges. The toughest was Sail-Maker's, followed by Martyr's. They hit sloops with tricks and turns around the Tappan Zee, plaguing them through Highlands to Newburgh Bay. Sharp winds off Croton Point could shred your sails. Many skippers suffered this fate, forcing them ashore at Haverstraw to see the sailmaker.

Martyr's Reach was worse. The Highlands Hills, the only part of the Appalachian Range crossed by a major river, force the mighty Hudson to bend at West Point. Skippers distracted with the tide and surface winds literally got sideswiped by gusts swooping down off those dangerously steep hills.

The lore of Germany's Rhine River trumpets ship-sinking dangers of the Lorelei. She's a beautiful siren who enchants river pilots. Luring in sailors with her promising charms, she wrecks ships on rocks hidden in the waters beneath her craggy hill. The Highlands, by comparison, rise from the Hudson River at more dramatic angles and to twice the height of the fabled German river mount. The Hudson River imp's death toll has been estimated at several hundred. These spirits, then, are just as formidable as the fabled Lorelei.

The skippers and crew strongly felt it took more than shifting wind and tide to topple their sloops. They believed imps, the spirits of those who had drowned in the Hudson, existed in the river's mists. Fail to "tip your hat" to them, and Dwerg, the Heer of Donder-Berg, trumpets out for his army of vengeful spirits. Grabbing gusts, they twirl head over heels north to a shadowy cove between Cro' Nest and Storm King. There, Mother Kronk, the witch of the Highlands, shakes her tablecloth to stir up a surprise storm. The Heer directs his troops to drive thunder, lightning, white-capped waves and shocking wind to sink the disrespectful skipper's vessel. Hundreds of sloops lie beneath the depths around "World's End." Marking the end of the world for all negligent skippers, it is, at 218 feet, the deepest spot on the river.

The Heer of Donder-Berg

Shipping companies occasionally assigned an ocean-going captain to "skipper" sloops to Albany. Once a greenhorn skipper took a look at the gaudily painted eighty-footer that he was ordered to pilot to Albany. Manned by a handful of Dutch-speaking sailors, the ship readied to transport rum. Shunning the bone-jangling week the journey could take on the Albany Post Road, folk Washington Irving dubbed "Knickerbockers" boarded the sloop. Descendants from of the original Nieuw Nederlanders, they preferred the flamboyant rather than the English fashions. Their skipper did not know a colorful ship had to be seen "in the offing" when the Hudson's fog crept up.

A band of sky-eyed, New York–born Dutchmen and one runaway slave, all wearing wooden shoes and billowy skilts, rolled aboard great wooden kegs of rum. Making like a sea captain on a brigantine, the new skipper barked out long orders.

"Grab hold the jib rope! Lower that boom! Stow our cargo! Get those Knickerbockers below!"

The old tiller man spoke up in a Dutch-accented English recognizable today as "Brooklynese." He let his skipper know his orders had already been carried out.

The skipper scoffed: "There's no mystery to this river! A child could sail it, and I shall rule it."

The crew widened their eyes. One whispered, "Our new Skipper is as headstrong as was old Peter Stuyvesant!"

"Yea, but he'll tip that feathered hat of his to the Heer of Donder-Berg!" declared the tiller man. "Or else de Imp will give him a peg leg!"

The crew hoisted up the leading jib, unfurled the main and raised the lofty skyscraper. Leaning hard on the tiller, they pushed off Manhattan Island. Wind caught the sails, rushing the sloop across the New York Harbor. The skipper shouted out orders, but the Knickerbockers stayed a step ahead of him.

Zigzagging from reach to reach, the skipper counted them out off his chart as they passed: "Great Chip Rock! Palisades! Tappan Zee! Haverstroo! Seyl-maker's…We are making headway!"

When the sloop wended its way by Stony Point, up stepped the tiller man. Pointing to a rippled dome of a mount across from Peekskill, the Dutch river man hollered: "Dondah-Boig! Youse must tip yer hat ta da Heer o' da Dondeh-Boig! He's master of these Highlands."

The skipper cried: "Tiller man! I shall tip my hat to old King George, to ladies fine and fancy, but never will I bow to foolish Dutch superstitions. I've sailed the seven seas! No river imp shall rule me!"

The tiller man tried a story to convince his skipper to tip the hat. Long ago, after one of Master Hendrick Hudson's sailor's, John Colman, took an arrow through the neck, he became a ghost known as Dwerg. Now he commands a troop of ghost-imps, all ready to sink any ship failing to show respect with a tip of its hat. Lower the skyscraper!

Still, the skipper dismissed the tale as nonsense. Hands of mist began swirling up from the river beneath the gnarled old hills. The sloop's crew now feared the ship's coming demise at World's End off West Point, where it seemed the river had no bottom.

Now if you only give the imps a glance, they appear as nothing more than mist or just a curl of fog. A closer inspection, however, reveals petrified faces peering through the gloom. The Mahicans knew them as manitous, or river spirits. Dutch settlers claimed they're the souls of those who have drowned in the Hudson. The Connecticut Yankees saw them as the lost crew of a ghost ship appearing on starless nights. Whatever they may be, they spirited up the Hudson Highlands. Mustering, the imps circle their Heer, Dwerg, the master-imp of Donder-Berg!

Dwerg glowered like an angry lord from atop a boulder at the disrespectful sloop. Wearing a doublet, bulbous breeches and a sugar loaf cap, he blasted out orders through his trumpet in low Dutch.

Legions of river spirits tucked head under heel to obey. Whirling their breezy fingers, they caught hold of the winds gusting off the mountains and

The Imp of Donder-Berg, 2008. *Photo by Todd Atteberry, www.thehistorytrekker.com.*

raced off to find their thunder. They blew above Bear Mountain and then pointed west to skitter beyond World's End. Shooting up at Crow's Nest, they dropped down into Mother Kronk's cove. There, under the shadow of Storm King Mountain, the misty imp brigades reported to the witch of the Hudson Highlands.

Covered in sturgeon scales, the ancient witch flashed her eyes toward the arriving sprites. Revealing two fish living in her eye sockets, she grinned and shook her aprons to roll out the thunder. Clouds roared and rolled. Jags of lightning exploded out of the witch's brew pot. She offered to trade her storm for the skipper's bones to add to her brew.

Dwerg's spirits raised up an anvil-headed thundercloud. They shoved it through the worregat to the Highlands. It cannonaded off the cliffs and crags, hitting the sloop, shivering its timbers. The Knickerbockers instinctively hauled down the sails. The imps got to the topsail before the crew, ripping it from the riggings! Churning their hands, they foamed up whitecaps on the river. Clouds crashed. The sloop listed toward the starboard side. Each time the skipper gave an order, the Heer countermanded him with thunder.

It looked like doom would greet them at World's End.

Defiant and gripping his tricorn hard on his head, the skipper insisted they'd weather the storm, bragging he'd been through far worse on the Atlantic.

A form appeared to perch on the bowsprit. "'Tis Dwerg!" shouted the tiller man. "De Master Imp o' Dondah-Boig!"

Squinting through the rain, the skipper refused to accept the Dutch imp. He claimed if anything supernatural boarded his ship, it could only be a water demon. The tiller man still urged his skipper to tip the hat. He refused. The skipper however, remembered an ancient tradition of calling upon a saint for help sailing. He ordered all hands on deck to offer a wish and a prayer for help from Saint Nicholas.

Now these were the days before Saint Nick gained fame for bringing toys to girls and boys. Indeed, Dutch New Yorkers knew of "Sint Heer Klaas." Every December 6, the dour-bearded bishop traveled on horseback to put treats and trinkets in children's shoes left out on the stoop. Back then, though, folks mostly called upon him for protection when traveling over waterways.

The Yorkers scrambled onto the rainy deck.

"Pray to Saint Nick!" shouted the skipper. "Get that demon off my ship!"

The raging thunder made believers of all. Obedient and humbled, everyone sang out the wish and the prayer: "Sint-Nicolaas! Behalve ons schip! (Oh, Saint Nick save our ship!)"

It may have been a spirit or a ghost, an imp or just a passing storm, but Dwerg was no demon! He would not leave. Enraged, he shot monster lightning and thunder at the ship. BA BA BOOM!!

The blast illuminated and reverberated through the Highlands. Tongues tied with terror. Wishes and prayers turned to gibberish!

The crew and passengers' twisted plea filled the imps with glee. Sides splitting, Dwerg laughed and chortled all the way back to his Donder-Berg boulder.

There, still chuckling, he figured the sloop had paid the imp toll in gales of laughter. The Heer of the Donder-Berg trumpeted off the storm. Imps with breezy fingers rolled up the thunder, buried the lightning and let the sun slant down, calming the river. The skipper, wringing rainwater from his frock coat, boasted.

"See, I told you we'd weather that storm! Imps do not rule me!"

The insult pricked the retreating Heer's pointy ears. Dwerg squeezed his face, raised his trumpet and blared. The horn sounded down the Donder-Berg and raced over Peekskill Bay to cross the water race by Garrison's Landing. The Master Imp caught up with the disrespectful ocean captain. Clipping off his feathered hat, Dwerg spirited it away.

Whisking and whirling, the imp gamboled the hat north for miles. He espied a church with a fingerling steeple. There he deposited the braggart's tricorn. Washington Irving claimed the town was in Esopus; other sources say Kingston. A higher look indicates the cap landed atop none other than the Church of Saint Nicholas in New Hamburg on Hudson.

Bareheaded as the bare bear of Bear Mountain, the hatless skipper slunk down below the decks. Next time that skipper, or any other who knew the Hudson's brine, reached Donder-Berg, he tipped hat, lowered the topsail and, to be sure, called for help from Sint Heer Klaas to safely pass by Donder-Berg! Dwerg remains the "Heer" and master of those Hudson Highlands.

SINT HEER KLAAS AND THE GODE FRAUV

The tradition of evoking Saint Nicholas when facing dangerous seas came across the ocean with the Dutch. They became a primarily Protestant nation after overthrowing Catholic Spain. Tolerant of other religions, they kept certain customs from their days under the Spanish yoke. The Dutch adored their "Sinter Klaas." But they adored their Holland even more.

When Henry Hudson returned to Europe with a land claim for the Netherlands, all the Dutch East India Company could establish were a few raw trading posts. Dutch folk, prospering from world trade, did not want to settle in the New Netherlands. So, they called on Saint Nicholas for help.

The reluctance of the Dutch to settle the New Netherlands forced the Dutch West India Company to accept an idea given to them by a woman. The *gode frauv*, or good wife, of one of the company suggested a ship go to the New World with Sinter Klaas. The men first scoffed: "How can you put a spirit on a ship?" The good woman explained, "Not the spirit, but the image of Sinter Klaas carved into the ship's mast." Desperate for colonists, the company agreed to try to lure them with a wooden figurehead.

They placed the wooden figure of the dour-robed and red-bearded bishop on the prow of a colony-bound ship. Adoring Sinter Klaas, new settlers boarded the ship assured of protection across the ocean. Once in New Amsterdam, however, they refused to stay on raw Manhattan until the skipper agreed to leave the ship's Sinter Klaas with them. The wooden Sinter Klaas stood for ages near the former fort and old Broadway. Wags even put tobacco into the saint's pipe and lit it for him. Good luck, healing smoke and visions came to all who breathed in the smoke of Sinter Klaas.

Granted, much of this legend was collected and retold by Washington Irving and his pal James Kirke-Pauling. No record has been found of the gode frauv or the Sinter Klaas ship. The tale still shows the roots of fear and wonder surrounding the lower Hudson Valley. Simply coming to the region required a little prayer to Saint Nicholas to appease the spirits.

THE AGENT AND THE IMPS

The folk traditions and legends of the Hudson River tell of imps, manitous or spirits inhabiting the Hudson River Highlands since precolonial times. Reports of these encounters, however, persist into the twenty-first century.

A real estate agent from Cold Spring on Hudson reported an unsettling encounter. Sailing with her husband, confident and comfortable at the helm of their sailboat, they slipped into the Hudson Highlands near Donderberg Mountain. Later she described what happened as an out-of-body experience.

The agent explained:

> *The market was very good in the nineties. We were able to buy a sailboat. We docked it down river, at Haverstraw Bay and always took it south toward New York harbor. We'd go out into Verrazano Narrows, even into the ocean. My husband handled anything the wind and tides threw at us. He loves it, and is quite an accomplished sailor.*
>
> *Well, one day, we decided to go north of Haverstraw Bay for a change. We wanted to sail by our home in Cold Spring. We never got there. We set out fine, maneuvering by Stony Point and the old lighthouse, beautifully. Jones Point and Kidd's Plug had some tricky tacking. I helped with the sails*

as we glided toward the Bear Mountain Bridge. I heard something about a pirate ship sinking and their ghosts spooking boats today.

The Realtor went on:

We passed by Donderberg, and there everything went wild. We didn't see it at first, but odd patches of fog swirled up from the river. The wind hit us from two different directions. My husband adjusted the sails. He did everything by the book. The boat took off in the wrong direction. He yelled, "I can handle this!" When he tried to bring us back, our boat spun around. We had no control over our sails. We decided to head back down river, just to get out of there.

It was like I could see us, as if from above, doing the right things, but our efforts had no effect on the boat. Sailing by Donderberg was an out-of-body experience. My husband, usually in control on the boat, just gave up completely flustered.

Following the event, she felt compelled to seek an explanation for something beyond wind, tide and sail. She had discovered the imps of Donder-Berg!

Oddly, the Highlands' dramatic beauty attracts relatively few boaters today. The Realtor's experience may not be unique. A schoolteacher from Ossining, New York, may have encountered what is truly more than the sum of wind, tide and storm on the Highlands:

My motorboat was suddenly surrounded by fog rising as we entered Peekskill Bay. Then a thunderstorm slammed us. The shores of the river just vanish into mists. I couldn't tell which direction I was headed. I was stunned finding myself genuinely scared. The whole thing then passed with surprising speed, blowing off my hat!

BERMUDA TRIANGLE ON THE HUDSON

Apparently, the Realtor and teacher were lucky. Christopher Letts, the Tarrytown Lighthouse keeper, fisherman and historian, speculates that hundreds of eighteenth- and nineteenth-century sailing sloops sank while trying to navigate the Hudson Highlands. "Sloops needed to make a profit," he explains.

"Undermanned, with a crew of maybe three or four, they were often over-loaded with lumber, hay, wheat, cows and all. This made them unwieldy and sinkable in a storm." There's more at play in the Highlands.

Thunderstorms, hidden by the Highlands, not only surprise powerboaters today but seem to descend upon them with unexpected speed. Reverberating off the craggy rocks like cannon shot, the storms envelop. Shocked to find their boat lost in a river squall, people describe a supernatural sensation.

Granted the tradition of tipping the hat or lowering your topsail rose from the savvy sailing needed to navigate through the tricky Hudson Highlands. Winds sweeping along the river and swooping down from the almost mountain-high hills clipped the sky-scraping sail while literally lowering the boom on the mainsail. Indeed, one poor sailor in 1866, according to the venerable book *Sloops on the Hudson*, had his head snapped off when a rogue wind got hold of a line. Early in the 1700s, Roger Brett, a British naval officer, was flummoxed by the wild Highland winds. They too caught hold of his boom, breaking his back, sending him under the ever-shifting waters of the Hudson and turning him into a local ghost. The frequency of sudden storms, disaster and death in the north of the Tappan Zee through the Highlands gives reason for people to look for an explanation beyond wind and tide. Imps on the Hudson appear plausible.

Today's Hudson River pilots are professionals who steer great diesel-powered ships up and down the river and know the river best. They keep the tradition of acknowledging the imps with a tip of their hats before chugging by Donder-Berg. The Rhine has its shipwrecking sirens. The Sargasso Sea swallows planes in its Bermuda Triangle. The Hudson, however, has its endangering, enduring imps.

THE SPUYTEN DUYVIL

The green skipper of yore was not the only one to see demons on the Hudson. Another bedeviling natural phenomenon called for a supernatural explanation. Once upon a time, Marble Hill sat on the very tip of Manhattan Island. The Harlem River looped around the little neighborhood to flow into the mighty Hudson. The ever-shifting waters where Manhattan meets the Bronx swirled wildly when the tide changed. Crossing the narrow Harlem at Marble Hill proved harrowing—timing mattered. Dutch settlers traveling in the mid-1600s from Manhattan to visit Jonas Bronck or Adrian Onder Donck called for Johannes Verveelen's ferry. If the tide was low, they waded across; when the tide changed, however, they witnessed whirlpools and water spurting between rocks. Sensing something beyond the powers of nature at work, the Dutch christened the river meeting "Spuitende Duivel," or spouting devil.

A bit of local lore reflects this feeling of something extraordinary there. Washington Irving, of course, took up accounts probably gleaned from Dutch New Yorkers. He tells of the indefatigable trumpeter to the director general of the New Netherlands, Anthony van Corlear. A barrel-chested, beer-swilling, flamboyant flirt, he served as "sounder of the brass" for all manner of alarms. This fellow's fame, however, stemmed from his prominent proboscis. Two birds could perch upon Anthony's nose and still there'd be room for a crow to sit.

One evening, Irving claims in *Diedrich Knickerbocker's History of New-York*, Van Corlear received a call to travel out from Manhattan to trumpet up the local militia. Other sources place Anthony visiting with Onder Donck. Traveling back to Manhattan, perchance to meet with one of his adoring ladies, he discovered a raiding party of English and Indians headed for an outpost in northern Manhattan. Needing whatever military help he could muster, Anthony sought out the Dane Jonas Bronck. He cajoled the good burgher out of bed, and Bronck gathered his freemen, servants and slaves upon the banks near the Spuitende Duivel. Verveelen the ferryman was not to be found. Recalling times he'd waded across, Van Corlear urged the Bronck men to follow his lead by swimming to Manhattan.

"What about the devil who dwells within these waters when the tide changes?" admonished Bronck. Here Irving claims Anthony van Corlear "swore most valorously that he would swim across in Spyt den Duyvel."

Plunging in the dark tide, Anthony swam, turned and beckoned to Bronck's company to join him. Anthony saw terror twist their faces. "Fear not mynheers! The water's fine." It was not the waters that frightened the Bronck men but rather the rising monster emerging behind unsuspecting Anthony. Irving describes it as a "duyvel in the shape of a huge moss-bonker." This creature was responsible for churning and spouting water when the tide pushed the rivers together. It may have snagged Anthony with immense crab claws or an unholy gaping mouth. Whatever means used, the devilish thing dragged the trumpeter under. Twice he fought back to the surface, while the Bronck men looked on paralyzed. Finally Anthony battled to get the brass horn to his lips. Blasting a warrior's attack call, he frightened off those besieging the Dutch fort. The English and Indians fully believed Peg Leg Peter Stuyvesant approached with his army.

The fort was saved. Alas, Anthony was not. The devil took him under the whirlpools and waterspouts. Anthony van Corlear left behind a lamentation of heartbroken ladies and a lasting legacy in the Bronx. A protective spirit now, his immense red nose appears in the Harlem River. On the occasion when someone dares to disrespect the Bronx, Anthony's ghost blasts a kind of raspberry on his trumpet—a sound known as the Bronx cheer!

In 1896, New York City opened the Harlem River Canal, closing off the river's turn around Marble Hill. Soon the remaining creek was filled in, connecting that part of Manhattan forever with the Bronx. The spitting devil—the spilling devil, speight den duyvil, spike and devil, spiten debill, the spouting spuyten duyvil of a devil and all the other names people called it over the centuries—disappeared. If ever a stalwart resident of Marble Hill hears someone say their neighborhood is in the Bronx, they scream: "To the devil with you! Marble Hill is part of Manhattan!"

VAN DAM, THE GHOSTLY ROWER

Keeping away the devil once meant keeping the Sabbath day. The Dutch Reformed and other colonial churches declared Sabbath at the stroke of midnight. Woe to any found dancing, drinking or cavorting thereafter!

Once during the days of the Dutch, a good man named Rambout van Dam hoped to get in a touch of revelry on a Saturday night. He promised the dominee that he'd keep the Sabbath and return to Kakait (New Hempstead, Rockland County) before the Reformed Church bell tolled.

Rambout rowed with the tide down to Spuyten Duyvil. There he drank and danced a jig with every lass he could. When the hour of eleven tolled, he begged the girls to let him leave—he'd made a promise to keep the Sabbath. They laughed, teasing that he had promised to meet yet another woman back across the Tappan Zee. Rambout left late, jumping into his boat and the changing tide holding up his oars. Pulling hard against the Hudson's tide, Rambout soon disappeared into the river's rising mists.

The fog closed about him, misty fingers reaching, tugging, cupping and keeping Rambout van Dam away from the west shore landing at Tappan Slote. The church bell tolled midnight, and Rambout had not been able

World's End, 1992 woodcut print. *By Vic Schwarz. Courtesy of the Vic Schwarz family through the Putnam County Museum & Foundry School Museum, Cold Spring, New York.*

to keep his promise. The river still keeps him forever rowing through the gloomy hours of Sunday morning.

Now Rambout has become a skeletal ghost in ragged clothes, trapped on the Tappan Zee. His eyeballs glow green with envy while all around people break the Sabbath. Crossing the Tappan Zee Bridge, while returning Sunday morning from Saturday parties, they rarely see the shroud of mist surrounding Rambout van Dam, the ghostly rower.

FLYING DUTCHMEN ON THE HUDSON

A legend from the ocean tells of a captain who cursed both God and devil in order to round Cape Horn. His ship made that stormy passage but for a fearful price. The captain and crew were doomed to sail forever, unless they could find a lass to fall in love with one of them. He would then gain freedom for the curse. Alas, the ship was granted landfall for just one night every seven years. Then, without love, they'd be condemned to sail another seven years.

The ship slipped across oceans, seas and wide rivers, never needing wind to fill its sails. An unearthly force powers the ship, known as the *Flying Dutchmen*. Some state they've seen it defying storms on the Tappan Zee.

The Redcoats once fired cannon upon it during the rebellion against King George. The shot went through the rigging and mast. Unscathed, the haunted vessel vanished. Once a man vowed he got off the *Dutchmen* at Tarrytown and stayed off when a tavern wench fell in love with him. He said he was the only sailor able to break the *Flying Dutchmen*'s spell in the seven landings he made. The ship traverses the Tappan Zee, while the crew screams for love in silenced voices.

Finally, who began bewitching Sleepy Hollow even as you approach on the Hudson River's Tappan Zee? Again, it's the spirited ghosts of those who failed to show respect for the river's vicissitudes. Entering the cove a touch north of Tarrytown, it's still best to evoke the blessed protection of old Saint Nicholas. And don't forget to tip your hat to the imps!

Chapter 4

MOTHER HULDA, THE HIGH GERMAN WITCH DOCTOR?

*Some say that the place was bewitched by a high German doctor, during the early days of the settlement (*TLSH, *4).*

Few legends can hold a candle to the iconic Headless Horseman. One figure, however, shines with a most unusual light. A kind yet strange soul, young Washington Irving learned of her while visiting the Old Dutch Church Cemetery. Her cottage once stood not far from the bridge where Ichabod Crane tried to dodge the galloping Hessian's hurled head. Irving omitted direct mention of her in *The Legend of Sleepy Hollow*. People nevertheless sense the presence of Mother Hulda, the witch.

Hulda lived as a solitary woman in the vicinity of Sleepy Hollow in the 1770s. A practicing herbalist, she bartered homemade medicine for some of her food and sundries. The Dutch farm folk shunned her as a stranger and a witch. Hulda redeemed herself during the American Revolution.

When esteemed historian Edgar Mayhew Bacon researched his 1898 book, *Chronicles of Tarrytown and Sleepy Hollow*, little had been written on Hulda. He relied, like Irving, on the great oral tradition, gathering lore from locals with memories stretching back to the 1830s. His anthology includes accounts with European origins given a local twist like the Legend of the Star Maiden. The name Hulda has roots in pagan Germany and Holland as a nature goddess. People in the German state of Hessen still refer to Hulda in an old expression. When it snows, they say, "Hulda's shaking her blanket," or they "slept under Hulda's blanket." Sometimes called Holda and Holle in pre-Christian times, she possessed knowledge of the weather, flax spinning and witchcraft. She was known at times as the "dark grandmother" and, coincidentally, as the White Lady. A Grimm Brothers fairy tale shows Mother Hulda with two daughters. One gets gold, the other pitch. Our Sleepy Hollow Hulda gets, in a way, a bit of both.

When a strange lone crone settled in Sleepy Hollow around 1770, she stirred up the Old World superstitions. A local historian, Mrs. Jack A. Dorland, the former national director of the Washington Irving Graveplot Restoration, noted in a 1975 article that when this newcomer arrived, the hamlet of Tarrytown grew ominously from twelve to thirteen families. Dorland described the times then as marked with xenophobia. The "dominee," or minister, named Ritzema admonished his congregation in the Old Dutch Church against having "foreign discourse," or conversation with the newcomer.

Dutch Americans before independence struggled to hold on to their language and culture with the wave of new settlers from New England and Germany sweeping into the lower Hudson Valley. Dutch rule along the Hudson may have ended in 1664 (with a brief return in 1673), but, as Washington Irving discovered, their ways lingered.

Based on Dorland, Bacon and other sources, the following is the story of Mother Hulda, the Witch of Sleepy Hollow and Tarrytown.

WITCH-DOCTOR-HEROINE

When the strange woman first appeared in Tarrytown's dry goods store, no one even tried to speak with her. Cloaked in a flowing shawl with deep-set eyes, the thin woman who looked Bohemian was shunned. She wasn't English, Dutch, German or even Indian. The Reverend Ritzema warned from the pulpit of the Old Dutch Church, "Do not have foreign intercourse." Strangers spelled trouble to this tightknit community.

Farmer Requa explained that he found her hut near Spook Rock. It was a place generally avoided. Legend had it that some Native curse made the stones moan. Searching for a lost cow, the thick scent of drying herbs drew him to Hulda's shack.

Then a local Weckquasgeek man, known for speaking several languages, entered the Tarrytown shop. Requa asked if he could speak to this stranger. The Native man asked the woman something. She replied in an unusual

Native dialect. He told the Dutchman she had come to live nearby and wished to barter her baskets, furs and medicines. Her name sounded like something from the Old World fairy tales. They called her Mother Hulda.

The Weckquasgeek man thought she had lived with a nearby tribe, perhaps the Siwanoy or Sint Sinct. She may have been a captive or a widow. Most of those tribes had died out or left the area.

He explained, "She's come to live with you Dutch people now." The Dutch folk declared her a witch.

Hulda's baskets were neatly woven and very sturdy. She always seemed to have a rabbit to trade with her neighbors. Farm folk always traded for fur. Nevertheless, the Dutch heeded the Reverend Ritzema's decree and remained circumspect. She may be a witch!

When people fell ill, however, with the croup, a wound or stomach pains, they'd discover a bundle of herbs on their stoops. They knew they came from the woman who practiced the art of healing with plants. Privately, they accepted Hulda's offerings, returning her favor with metal goods like needles, betty lamps or cooking pots. Publicly, they scoffed, claiming, "I take no yarbs from that Mother Hulda!"

The American Revolution tore Westchester County in half. The Patriots took the upper part above the Croton River. The Tories held the lower part below White Plains. Tarrytown and Sleepy Hollow remained in the "Neutral Grounds"—a no-man's land. There some took sides, marching off to fight. Everyone feared both armies. Raiders for the British, called "Cow-boys," plundered many a farm. "Skinners," their American counterparts, did the same. Farmers hid their cattle on a nearby ragged rise, sometimes milking the cows there and even churning butter. Thus it earned the name Buttermilk Hill. Hulda often foraged there as well, much to the chagrin of the war's thieves.

The war made folk in the area all the more appreciative of Hulda's bundles. Raid victims received, along with homemade medicine, bundles of dried rabbit meat, edible roots and even an occasional maple syrup sweet, all compliments of Mother Hulda. Now no one pretended to reject Hulda's gifts. Her medicinal plants proved a special godsend with the pox of war upon them. Still few people directly acknowledged Hulda even in those trying times. They feared the Reverend Ritzema's warnings. The herb woman had to face the horrors of war with no one to comfort her.

The fight came to Tarrytown on October 4, 1776. Redcoats landed ashore from an expeditionary fleet in the Tappan Zee. Apparently they sought rebel supply houses, forage and maybe some "Cow-Boy cattle."

Daniel Martling roused the local Minutemen to ready some small cannons. Irving, in *The Legend*, describes him as "Doffue Martling," boasting about how he fired off at the British warships until his gun burst. Tarrytown actually gave in to the British force without firing a shot. The local militia not only declined Hulda's services as a sharpshooter but also made a hasty retreat at the sight of the Redcoats.

The American War of Independence put Tarrytown in the dangerous no-man's land. This meant raids and skirmishes plagued the region. The historic record shows another British raid the following year. Official accounts from both sides recorded no military deaths, but one did occur.

Returning from a medicine delivery near Battle Hill in White Plains, Hulda happened upon the raid. British troops again landed from *The Phoenix* and *The Rose*, their warships in the Tappan Zee. Tarrytown militiamen nervously mustered and were forming a line to make a stand. Terrified by the well-armed Regulars, the local rebels dared not fire. Hulda dashed to her hut, gathered her musket and powder horn and took a position on the front line.

The Old Dutch Church sexton, there among the militia ranks, reported it was Hulda who broke the standoff. When the British spied the Dutch sharpshooter, they sent dragoons out to stop her. Hulda lived up to her ancient name as a wood goddess. She not only eluded the pursuing Redcoats, the bewitching Patriot got them lost, drawing them away from Tarrytown.

When the shooting stopped and the British returned to their vessels, out came the Dutch Minutemen of Tarrytown, minus their top shot. Striding a short distance east of the Old Dutch Church, they found the lank, lifeless body of Mother Hulda. No silver bullet required for killing this "witch." A mere ball of lead pierced her humble body. The one they thought of as being dark as pitch proved to have for them a brave heart of gold.

No one knew what to do. Hulda had acted heroically, but they considered her a pagan witch. They feared touching the body; some thought it was safer to leave her to the elements. "She must be buried!" Requa and others insisted.

A few people searched her hut and discovered a Bible and a will calling for gold to be given to war widow families. "She acted like a good Christian!" a good wife declared. "She drove off those Redcoats for us!" They wrapped her body in her shawl and carried it to the Old Dutch Church Graveyard.

"She cannot be placed in sacred church ground," Dominee Ritzema explained. "She is not Christian!"

They decided to show their heroic witch respect. Ritzema allowed the body buried away from the marked Christian graves. The Witch of Sleepy

Hollow was laid to rest by the north wall of their Old Dutch Church. Ritzema left the grave unmarked. Hulda, however, made her mark on Sleepy Hollow during those trying times. She's the "high German doctor" who left a spell on Sleepy Hollow.

WHITE CAPTIVES

Country people of the eighteenth century in Europe and America commonly called widows living alone and over the age of fifty witches. Hulda, though an exceptional woman, was no exception to this rule. Anyone, especially a single woman, coming into a small community would suffer exclusion. A white woman speaking an Indian language indicated "native captivity." This resulted from the clashes of colonial cultures. The times brought disease, skirmishes and war. Occasionally after raiding settlements, the Native people took in the orphaned children of the Europeans and Africans. Some were ransomed. Others, like Tarrytown's Hulda and the daughter of the Westchester pioneer Anne Hutchinson, integrated into the Native community.

Anne Hutchinson was killed by a Weckquasgeek war party in 1643 during the Willem Kieft wars. Her daughter, Hannah, abducted by the tribe, became part of their community. Several years later, when the girl was in her teens, Peter Stuyvesant managed to ransom her. She soon chose, however, to return to live among Native peoples, marrying an Esopus man. Hulda, a Native-speaking white woman, apparently shared Hannah's fate. Taken, or taken in, she probably had a Native husband who died, leading the Native folk to return her to a European community.

Bacon describes Hulda as a Bohemian. Curiously, the Philipse family originally descended from the ancient Viscounts Felyps of Bohemia. This choice of ethnic background evokes the old stereotype given to the Romany or Gypsy peoples from Bohemia, a province in the Czech Republic, on the German border. Bohemian gypsies were considered eccentric and untrustworthy by their Slavic and Germanic neighbors. Hulda certainly fell victim to those fears.

New York's Last Witch Trial

Labeling newcomers witches continued to be a local Dutch practice along the Hudson right into the early nineteenth century. The last witch trial in New York took place around 1815 in an equally xenophobic Dutch community near Nyack. Naut Kanniff, widow to a Scottish Presbyterian minister, arrived to the same shun and chagrin that welcomed Mother Hulda to Sleepy Hollow. Dressed not in Dutch drab but in colorful calico with flowing hair, she too had nature's touch for the healing herbs. The local Dutch people targeted her as a witch. When butter didn't churn and cows broke loose, a mob demanded that Naut Kanniff be tried for this witchcraft.

A judicious judge ruled "good will outweigh evil. Place her on a scale against a brass bound Bible from old Holland." The crowd complied. The woman went down, where a witch would have flown up. Disappointed, the folks of Nyack had no witch to drown.

Widows vilified as witches plagued Sleepy Hollow and, indeed, the Hudson Valley. Irving reminds us, in another *Sketch Book* story called

Bridge near the Old Dutch Church, 2009. *Photo by Todd Atteberry, www.thehistorytrekker.com.*

Above: The Headless Horseman of Sleepy Hollow, circa 1842–65 oil on canvas. *By George Washington Allston Jenkins, Historic Hudson Valley, Tarrytown, New York; Gift of Benjamin G. Jenkins (ss.64.538 a-b).*

Below: Headless Horseman and Ichabod at the bridge, 1876 illustration. *From* Harper's Monthly, *April 1876. From the collection of the Highland Studio, Inc., Cold Spring, New York.*

Headless Horseman chasing Ichabod Crane, 1858 oil on canvas. *By John Quidor, Smithsonian Institution Collection, Washington, D.C.*

Lighthouse near Caldwell's Landing, circa 1850 oil on canvas. *By Edmund Coates. Permission of the Family of Edward A. Vrooman through the Putnam County Historical Society and Foundry School Museum, Cold Spring, New York.*

Headless Horseman in Pursuit of Ichabod Crane, circa 1870 watercolor on paper. *By Felix O.C. Darley, Historic Hudson Valley, Tarrytown, New York (ss.80.26).*

Hesse-Cassel Corps of Field Jaegers, 2007, oil on panel. *By Don Troiani, www.historicalimagebank.com.*

Left: Ichabod Crane and Katrina van Tassel, 1861 oil on canvas. *By Daniel Huntington, Historic Hudson Valley, Gift of Vanderbilt Webb and William H. Osborn (PM.71.2 a-b).*

Below: The Capture of Major Andre, 1834. Unknown (after Asher B. Durand), oil on canvas. *Historic Hudson Valley (ss.82.2 a-b).*

Above: Old Dutch Church from Albany Post Road, 2008. *Photo by Todd Atteberry, www.thehistorytrekker.com.*

Below: Old Dutch Church at Sleepy Hollow, 1861 oil on canvas. *By William Rickarby Miller, Historic Hudson Valley (P.M. 79.3).*

Above: *Sunnyside. By George Inness, Historic Hudson Valley.*

Left: The Headless Hessian, Philipsburg Manor, Sleepy Hollow, 2008. *Photo by Bryan Haeffele, Historic Hudson Valley.*

"Wolfert's Roost," that witches and spirits never really leave Sleepy Hollow: "In a remote part of the Hollow, where the Pocantico forced its way down rugged rocks, stood Carl's Mill, the haunted house of the neighborhood…a goblin-pile…A horseshoe nailed to the door to keep off witches, seemed to have lost its power."

A woman shunned in spite of her helpful herbs and heroics and buried in an unmarked grave remains a presence and power in Sleepy Hollow today. Visitors ask about Hulda the Witch, and the local historical society can provide directions to the site of her hovel. When Washington Irving wandered through in the late 1790s and early 1800s, doubtlessly he learned of the bewitchment. There's a sense of Mother Hulda in that spell cast by the "high German witch doctor."

The original haunting of Sleepy Hollow sprang forth from the gloom formed around the Hokohonkgus tree when intertribal war left corpses like stones unburied. The Native ghosts groaned out of their graves when turned out and trampled over by the Dutch. They gave way to the British who left for the rebelling Americans the spirits of Sleepy Hollow: "The immediate cause, however, of the prevalence of supernatural stories in these parts was doubtless owing to the vicinity of Sleepy Hollow. There was a contagion in the very air that blew from that haunted region. It breathed forth an atmosphere of dreams and fancies infesting all the land" (*TLSH*, 53).

Chapter 5

WOMEN IN WHITE

Some mention was made also of the woman in white, that haunted the dark glen at Raven Rock, and was often heard to shriek on winter nights before a storm, having perished there in the snow (TLSH, *31*).

STORM SHRIEKERS

Distinguished folklorist Edgar M. Bacon in 1897 created a careful chronicle of the ghosts infusing the air about Sleepy Hollow. Sleepy Hollow High School students from Ms. Cecelia Kingston's folklore classes continued the quest. Researching the local oral tradition in the late 1970s, they compiled a terrific anthology of stories. All historians and folklorists of the region encounter tales tangled up with the works of Washington Irving. He only gives "some mention" to the ghost crying before storms. The evanescent Woman in White, however, remains widely reported.

Reminiscent of various powerful fairies called White Ladies once spotted throughout northern Europe, the Sleepy Hollow howlers adapted to their unique surroundings. The earliest shrieks rise along Raven Rock, an isolated glacial scar on Buttermilk Hill. The jagged thirty-foot ledge first made a manitou, or spirit, of a Weckquasgeek woman eluding rape. Later a Dutch farm wife perished there in a blizzard. Bacon speaks of a "Woman of the Cliff, who flits along on the top of the rocks on a certain ledge that overlooks the village." A female voice rising from the hill foretells of winter storms with a keening call. People today maintain there's a presence of a woman's spirit, "hovering near Raven Rock," "crossing over the cemetery floating toward the river," "appearing as firelights" and "giving unearthly moans" before bad weather. The strongest shrieks emanate from a lovelorn lady who fell in the no-man's land of central Westchester during the American Revolution.

A scrupulous "collecting and collating of the floating facts," along with a study of the tradition of tales concerning the storm shrieking lady, yields the next stories.

MANITOU

When the Hokohonkgus tree had scarcely grown beyond the saplings, a man ruled by desire, not love, pursued a woman not of his tribe. He did not court her with wampum belts, furs or sweet songs. So she refused to give him even a word.

Enraged, he decided that if she would not have him, then no one would have her. He demanded she come to him. She ran away from the Mahicanituck to the fields above Pocantico's dancing waterfall. He hunted her like an animal. Passing the place of the skulls near Council Rock, she began losing ground. Near the immense rock standing off from the cliff, she prayed, "Great Manitou, help me!"

The ravens there carried her prayers to the creator spirit. The man drew an arrow from his quiver and aimed it in his bow. She clambered onto the great rock, and in full trust, she leapt off into the air.

The creator spirit sent ravens to catch up and turn her into a manitou. Her spirit, like a protective mist, inhabits the place now called Raven's Rock.

THE SPIRIT SAINT OF RAVEN ROCK

Shortly after Hulda built a hovel near the Pocantico in the 1770s, a poor farm wife stepped into more woe in Sleepy Hollow. This woman sensed snow in the clouds hanging over the Tappan Zee. She desperately needed wood to weather the gathering storm. Still, something told her to stay inside. The air inside the cottage, however, felt brittle with cold. Sighing, she tied her thick wool shawl beneath her chin, grabbed the wood sack and stepped into the failing sun.

She noticed the Pocantico tumbling over stones as if anxious to reach the Hudson. The bell on the Dutch Church tolled a muffled note in the winds now pushing off the river. The church sexton appeared. The farm wife nodded.

"Not a-gathering wood now are you?"

"Just enough for the night," she replied.

"Some good branches just fell near Raven Rock."

"It's not too far."

The farm wife collected a fagot of chestnut just after the Hokohonkgus Tree and added some pine from near Spook Rock. She spied Mother Hulda's cottage. Remembering the medicine bundle of willow and yarrow the witch had left a few days ago, the farm wife dropped her fagot of wood on the witch's stoop. No need to visit; Hulda was shy about company.

Walking off toward Raven Rock, she heard the witch's door creak open. Hulda beckoned her in for tea.

"No thank you kindly, Mother Hulda. I need to gather more wood before this blizzard catches us."

These were the days when farmers clear cut, leaving only the great trees standing. Folks scoured the forest floor for firewood. Limbs often fell around Buttermilk Hill. Hulda admonished her visitor against going there. "No need to worry, Mother Hulda. I know these woods as well as you."

But the snow and wind conspired against the wood gatherer. They turned the trail and trees into a shadowy maze. One hulking form of rock dared show itself through the storm. A squall of snow drove her to seek shelter there. She crouched down against the stone, hoping to wait it out. Raven Rock felt dense and stifling. Blanketing snow induced a drowsy, dangerous enchantment. She could not shake the cold from her weary bones. Sleep became intoxicating.

Once her body was laid to rest in the Dutch Church yard, the spell of Sleepy Hollow granted her one thing. Whenever the Tappan Zee conjures up snowstorms, her spirit coalesces. If the wind stirs up enough ash, river mist and decomposing leaves, she reappears. Giving shape to the already moving airs, she keens and wails warnings to travelers. The Woman of the Cliff dislikes frightening the living, but better they flee away from storms near Raven Rock than suffer her cold fate. The locals still heed her cries.

THE WHITE LADY OF RAVEN ROCK

Wind pushing off the Tappan Zee sometimes carries an eerie voice. It ululates a harbinger of the coming storm and tells of a forlorn spirit, the White Lady of Raven Rock.

British officers, after the Battle of White Plains, sought out houses along the shores of the Hudson to serve as quarters while awaiting orders from General William Howe. Two grenadiers appeared on the stoop of a rough-hewn cottage near Sleepy Hollow. The younger, a handsome lieutenant, went to knock but his superior, a gruff major, stopped him. He ordered the younger officer to observe. The older soldier lifted the latch. The pair tromped in, mud and manure falling from their boots. The major announced: "By the power granted to us soldiers of his majesty George the Third, we your protectors from Washington and his rebel mob, give you the privilege of quartering us in this house...Come forward and be of service to your King!"

No one appeared.

The lieutenant pointed to a fire crackling in the hearth. The major ordered.

"Come forward and serve your King!"

Now, behind a flour barrel, trembled a young woman—her name may have been Gertje, but no one now tells. She hoped the officers, upon seeing her humble home, would leave. Recalling the other Westchester homes burned by the Hessians for the British army, she wisely came out from her hiding.

"Forgive me sir, I am much afeared!"

"Nothing to fear save those d——d rebels!" exclaimed the major. He asked if she was alone. She explained she lived in Sleepy Hollow with her brothers. They were off fighting. "One for our king and one for the rebels," she carefully stated. He ordered her to be of some service by removing their boots and preparing some supper.

Gertje gripped the major's filthy boots and pulled them off. The lieutenant noticed her delicate hands. Even covered with mud, they were beautiful. He decided to remove his own boots outside. Gertje smiled at the lieutenant and said she could only give them hasty pudding and brown bread.

The lieutenant smiled back, replying, "'Tis better than Saint Anthony's meal!" Thus began their love.

The commander of these two Redcoat officers, General Howe, fought like a slow game of chess. He cogitated troop movements over wine, hoping Washington's ragtag force would surrender before facing all the artillery pieces, Hessian knights and field army pawns. This gave the lieutenant time with his Sleepy Hollow Lady.

The two spent hours strolling along the shores of the Tappan Zee talking of times of peace. The lieutenant waxed on about his family's sugar plantation on the peaceful island of Jamaica. His Dutch American sweetheart no doubt longed to be taken away from war-torn Westchester.

The major laughed at the younger officer, advising him to enjoy the colonial wench, "for soon we all will march and be fated to die!"

The neighbors did not see any joy in Gertje's falling for a British officer.

The blacksmith, Martling, confided to the alewife in Van Tassel's tavern. One afternoon he found the two of them behind the shop, holding hands. The alewife thought this a trifle, considering she had caught the two of them kissing by the river. They considered the couple doomed.

One day, the war beckoned. A messenger from General Howe came to the door of Gertje's cottage, ordering the officers to report to Dobbs Ferry to pursue Washington and his rebels in New Jersey. The major advised the lieutenant to bid his colonial wench farewell, adding with a smirk, "Give her a kiss for me."

The lieutenant dashed off to find his love, begging her to come with him. Gertje worried about her love's urgency. He took her to Raven Rock, a craggy outcrop high above the gloom of Sleepy Hollow.

There they took in the wide Tappan Zee, with the cliffs of the Palisades stretching down to New Jersey. She wondered why they were here.

At once, the lieutenant dropped on bended knee. He took Gertje's hand and asked, "Whilst thou marry me?" She gasped. He went on, "I shall leave the service of the King, to sail here to take thee away to Jamaica where we shall enjoy only peace."

Gertje kissed both of her love's cheeks and answered, "I shall marry thee. I will make a gown of white! And await you here!"

"Splendid!" cried the lieutenant. "Come in two months time when my service is done. I will sail through the Tappan Zee to Tarrytown. Look from this rock for my white topsail!"

The couple departed with a last kiss, believing in love's enduring protection.

The lieutenant and major rejoined General Howe. How they fought against George Washington and his blue coats! Gertje, meanwhile, gathered scraps of white wool, linen and linsey-woolsey. She pieced, patched and sewed her wedding gown.

Blacksmith Martling told the lass neither of her brothers could ever accept her eloping with a British officer. He warned the lieutenant wanted only steal kisses and something more precious! Van Tassel's alewife worried the officer would leave Gertje crying! The young woman insisted her love was true.

When exactly two months had passed, Gertje appeared in a patchwork gown of white on Raven Rocks. Peering out over the Tappan Zee, she spied not her beloved's white sail but the first storm of winter. Steely clouds massed over the Palisades. White caps roiled on the Hudson River. Bitter winds pushed icy snow toward Raven Rock.

Gertje, hoping for her love, saw the foamy waves fluttering like a white sail. She called, "My Beloved! Is that you? Have you come for me?"

Only the stinging snows and biting winds answered. Gertje looked out again. When white caps appeared, she saw sloop sails. The freezing lass continued to call.

"My Beloved! Is that you? Have you come for me?"

Only the stinging snows and biting winds answered. Still, Gertje stayed on the cliffs near Raven Rocks. The winds pushed through her gown. The snows stung her cheeks, blistered bloody her lips and left her delicate beautiful hands raw with frostbite. Searching for her love, she cried out until her voice grew hoarse.

"My Beloved! Is that you? Have you come for me?"

Only the stinging snows and biting winds answered.

"The course of true love, never did run smooth" the wise Bard wrote, "but, either was it different in blood!"

Where was the lieutenant? Dead on a New Jersey battlefield? Some claim the major prevented the disgrace elopement of a gentleman British officer and rebellious Yankee doodle of a wench. Thus he locked up the lieutenant.

When morning came, the White Lady was gone. Had her beloved come? Or had the snow and war swept her away? Months later, when her brothers returned to Sleepy Hollow, the alewife explained their sister's absence as a love gone wrong, forcing the lass to hide in shame in New York City.

The blacksmith agreed: "The lieutenant, he stole kisses then broke Gertje's heart!" Spring, however, gave the answer.

Two huntsmen hoping to find rabbit at Raven Rock found instead a strange misshaped form. Shocked at a frozen form revealed under the melting snow, they dashed down from the craggy hill and burst into the Old Dutch Church.

"Dominee! We found something up at Raven Rock! Come see and bring your Good Book."

The good man grabbed his Bible and followed the hunters. There the dominee clapped eyes on a wretched figure mingled with the snow.

Apparition of the White Lady at Raven Rock, Sleepy Hollow, New York, 2007. *Courtesy of photographers Brian Haffele, Historic Hudson Valley, and Todd Atteberry, www.thehistorytrekker.com.*

He recognized hands that once removed the filthy boots of a British trooper. Now, he saw those knuckles breaking through the frozen skin. He remembered those cheeks once flush like peaches. Ice had torn them off the jawbone. He recalled those lips speaking defiantly of love; he cringed at their broken blisters. Alas, this once was dear Gertje who loved a British officer. Did a Yankee bullet take her love? Was it the major's disapproval? She held her vigil at Raven Rock through a blizzard, but only grim death came for her.

Gertje's homespun wedding gown turned into a funeral wrap. The dominee had her body laid to rest by the Old Dutch Church. Her forlorn spirit, however, remains restless. Rising before ill weather, the White Lady returns to haunt the cliffs overlooking Tarrytown. Her shrieks now mark the coming of a storm. Old-timers say the source of her power is found in the dominee's Good Book. There in Solomon's psalms, it states, "Love is as strong as Death; jealousy is cruel as the grave."

The strength of the lady's love now lifts her from the cruel grave, moving her through the mists and gloom of Sleepy Hollow. Her spirit caught in love's spell, her voice caught in the wind, still laments "My Beloved! Have you come for me?"

WITTE JUFFERN OF SLAAPER'S HOL

The mention made in *The Legend* of the White Lady's warning cries, hints of her shape shifting in the snow and pelting Ichabod Crane with "witch tokens," indicates something deeper than ghosts at play. Our wailing woman echoes Irish lore of the "Bean Si" (Banshe) who screams before a death. Katherine Briggs, in her *Encyclopedia of Fairies*, notes White Ladies are a mix between fairy and ghost. Specifically, the Dutch version, known in Holland as "Wiite Juffern," commonly dwelled in cavelike shelters near small towns. Our White Lady takes up such a residence at Raven Rock.

The presence of several melancholy protective entities near "Slaaper's Hol" gives evidence of Dutch fairy tale traditions in Washington Irving's *Legend*, and in regional lore as well. They are similar to the ship-sinking imps of the Hudson Highlands. Both are spirits of the dead acting in fairylike roles.

Fairy tale traditions transported from Europe to America, like folk music, were adapted to the new landscape. Once upon a time, in the Old World, people left fields fallow for the little people. Peasants gave gifts in return for medicine from the fairies. Caves and crags were left open for the ancient enchanted races. Passersby sang psalms to ward off those old ones. The New World, especially around Sleepy Hollow, developed its own cautionary ways. Thus tip your hat to salute the imps of Donder-Berg. Sing a psalm like Ichabod Crane's to frighten away ghosts. And heed the wailings of the White Lady who cries before coming storms.

The protective nature spirits of Old World White Ladies reappear indeed in Sleepy Hollow's folklore. Originally these nature fairies captivated lovers, gave gifts of precious stones and spread seeds that eventually became spirits of the wind. Around Sleepy Hollow, heartbreak led them to sound storm warnings.

The primordial White Lady emerges in another epic story: the Legend of King Arthur. The chieftain who first united tribal Britain against Saxon invaders had a "white phantom" or "apparition" of a wife. Guinevere translates from the ancient Brythonic as "Gwenhwyvar," meaning white ghost. Clearly, Arthur's queen foreshadows Sleepy Hollow's White Ladies.

Across the ocean, colonists frightened by the wilderness felt something unearthly in the winds off the Hudson. There's a Native story of an aggravated young woman transformed, like a New World Daphne, into a manitou. Following her to Raven Rock, some European women ignore or miss the Native spirit's warning. They become fairy-ghosts themselves, wailing new warnings in the wind.

The Dutch settlers of the lower Hudson Valley may have been the "hard blond traders" described by Carl Carmer. Pragmatists when facing the raw wilderness, strange Native peoples and rival European powers, the Dutch also encountered things unknown. They never experienced the dense forests, jagged palisades and misty coves found along the Hudson. The Tappan Zee's sudden sail-sheering wind, the moaning in the hills and the gloomy atmosphere turned them back to folklore from home for explanations. Thus new phenomena encountered in the New Netherlands made White Ladies at Raven Rock, imps in the Highlands and other spirits too.

Finally, the collection of spirit lore that Ms. Cecelia Kingston's class gathered indicate Sleepy Hollow remains a place fraught with "marvelous tales of ghosts and goblins, and haunted fields, and haunted brooks, and haunted bridges, and haunted houses." One relatively recent report, however, shows a return of some Old World fairy tale. The son of John D. Rockefeller Jr., son of one of the richest men of all time, found Raven Rock romantic. Sunshine and lush foliage with a river view made his "secret love-seat." Raven Rock today rises above the noise and dense suburban development of Westchester County. Apparently, the White Lady restored it to idyllic fairy refuge: "If ever I should wish for a retreat, whither I might steal from the world and its distractions, and dream quietly away the remnant of a troubled life, I know of none more promising than this little valley" (*TLSH*, 3).

Chapter 6

"THE TRAGICAL STORY OF THE UNFORTUNATE ANDRE"

It was connected with the tragical story of the unfortunate Andre, who had been taken prisoner hard by; and was universally known by the name of Major Andre's tree. The common people regarded it with a mixture of respect and superstition, partly out of sympathy for the fate of its ill-starred namesake, and partly from the tales of strange sights, and doleful lamentations, told concerning it (TLSH, 60).

The Hudson River served as the stage for nation-shaping ordeals during the American Revolutionary War. Decisive battles along the upper river near Saratoga provided "the turning point of the Revolution." Significant clashes occurred at Harlem Heights, Pelham, White Plains, Stony Point, the Hudson Highlands and Kingston. The lower Hudson Valley endured terrible raids by both Loyalist Cow-Boys and Patriot Skinners. When George Washington declared West Point on the Hudson "the key to the continent," both Congress and the British agreed. Two immense chains were stretched across the river to figuratively and literally hold the new nation together. Redcoat forces under General Sir Henry Clinton cut the first like a "Yankee pumpkin vine." Links later set by the Polish Patriot and engineer Thaddeus Kosciuszko held against British warships like "Washington's watch chain." When Washington's best fighting general, Benedict Arnold, turned traitor, he slipped that strategic key to the entire American bid for independence to a young British major disguised as a traveling merchant. Thus beneath branches of a Sleepy Hollow tulip tree unfolds the tragic story of John Andre.

The tale of Arnold and Andre remains the most intriguing event of the American Revolution, especially to those in the Hudson Valley. Today the region has two Andre monuments, an Andre Brook, a historic trail and a memorabilia room devoted to the incident at Sleepy Hollow's historical society. Now, around Halloween, an animatronic effigy of John Andre is hanged at Philipseburg Manor. Every hamlet and house Andre visited on his fateful journey boasts a marker, a plaque and a story. Further, John Andre's ghost pervades the area, particularly in Sleepy Hollow.

A Tragic Story Unfolds

He organized an intrepid assault on Quebec, helped commandeer Fort Ticonderoga, saved the American cause at Lake Champlain and heroically led American forces to victory at Saratoga. Benedict Arnold had horses shot out from under him, suffered bullet wounds to the leg and was arguably the new nation's top fighting general. Congress, however, belatedly recognized Arnold's battlefield prowess. They actually court-martialed him for using troops to move his personal goods in Philadelphia. George Washington "would have been much happier in an occasion of bestowing commendations" on Arnold. Congress ordered their commander in chief to reprimand Arnold's actions as "imprudent and improper." Feeling overlooked and outraged, Arnold believed Congress ruined the Revolution and his career. His young Loyalist wife, Peggy Shippen, then suggested Arnold go turncoat. The jilted general agreed. Peggy sought help from an old flame, the British adjutant general, Major John Andre. They conspired in 1780 to make Arnold a British general, hand America's fortress at West Point to the Redcoats and put an end to the foolhardy American bid for independence.

Handsome, ruthless, endearing, ambitious, artistic and careless, John Andre coordinated and executed the plot. Tragically, misfortune and miscalculation marred Andre's every move. Still, this genteel British officer came tantalizingly close to accomplishing his mission. Alas, three Skinners caught the fated major a few miles from his destination. They apprehended him right beneath a huge tree on the Sleepy Hollow/Tarrytown line. Andre suffered the hangman's noose. Arnold made brigadier, plus £6,315 sterling. The Revolution succeeded.

Ghost hunters claim they may detect a supernatural presence when someone dies unjustly or with unfinished business. John Andre's strange case meets both criteria. This rising officer felt Arnold and circumstance induced him to act like a spy. Many like Alexander Hamilton and the Marquis de Lafayette agreed. They put forth Andre as a man worthy of a far better fate.

The visionary nineteenth-century writer George Lippard, in his *Washington & His Generals, or Legends of the Revolution*, said:

> *Arnold escapes the hand of vengeance now. No, flushed with triumph, he goes on to complete his career of blood. He will gather gold—renown, aye favor from the hands of his King. But in the hour of his proudest triumph, even when he stands beside the Throne, one form, invisible to all other eyes, will glide through the thronging courtiers, and wither him, with its pale face, its white neck polluted by the gibbet's rope, its livid lip trembling with a muttered curse—the Phantom of John Andre!*

John Andre, the up-and-coming officer, was distinguished by unswerving service on the battlefield and inspiring performances on stage. Born in London to French Huguenot parents and raised in a merchant's home, Andre excelled at various arts and languages. Heartbroken after the family of his beloved, Honora Sneyd, rejected his marriage proposal, Andre bought an officer's commission in the British army. He shipped out with the regiment sent to quell restless New England colonies in the early 1770s.

Andre fought bravely in Canada against American forces under Generals Richard Montgomery and Benedict Arnold. Captured and held in grim conditions, Andre soured on the rebellious colonists. He wrote in a letter to his friend, the poet Anna Seward, complaining that Americans "stripped [me] of everything except the picture of Honora, which I concealed in my mouth. Preserving this yet [I] think myself fortunate." A prisoner of war exchange in Pennsylvania returned Andre to active duty serving as an aide to Major General Charles Grey. He participated in "No-Flint" Grey's bayonet-driven assaults on American forces at Brandywine, Germantown and Monmouth and at massacres in Old Tappan and Paoli.

During the British occupation of Philadelphia in the summer of 1778, Andre wrote, costumed and designed a theatrical extravaganza called the *Mischianza*. There he engaged in a flirtatious relationship with Peggy Shippen, an irresistible Tory eighteen-year-old. The next year, however, she married thirty-eight-year-old General Benedict Arnold.

Andre's efforts in both the theaters of war and stage soon earned him the post of adjutant general under Sir Henry Clinton, commander of Britain's

North American forces. When her new husband soured on Congress and the American Revolution, Peggy knew just who to contact. John Andre could help with her disgruntled Benedict.

BETRAYING BENEDICT

Benedict Arnold in America is a synonym for traitor. In September 1780, after years of valiant fighting for American independence, Arnold abandoned his new country and comrades. He accepted his enemy's offer to become a brigadier general. Scholars, historians and folklorists in the Hudson Valley still debate why Arnold became a turncoat. Many state that had Arnold not switched sides, his heroics would have ranked second only to George Washington's.

During the war's first years, Benedict Arnold not only fought with distinction, but he also secured the new United States. He led, along with Ethan Allen, the attack on Fort Ticonderoga. While Allen held a drunken victory celebration with his Green Mountain Boys, Arnold commandeered the cannons that Henry Knox later hauled to defend Boston. Arnold spearheaded daring and arduous assaults on Quebec City and Montreal. His brilliant tactics at naval battle of Valcour Island prompted historian Alfred T. Mann to declare, "When Benedict Arnold on Lake Champlain by vigorous use of small means, obtained a year's delay for the colonists, he compassed the surrender of Burgoyne in 1777."

Arnold's brash leadership on the battlefields near Saratoga and his countersiege against St. Legers' attack on Fort Stanwix foiled the famed British "three-pronged attack." A strategy devised by General John Burgoyne to divide the colonies along the Hudson River, Arnold stopped two of the three British assaults. Granted, the other American commander at Saratoga, General Horatio Gates, benefited from carefully planned fortifications and troop placements made by Kosciuszko. It was Arnold, however, on a brown charger, who literally led the most decisive attack. American Continentals and militia alike found courage to fight by following Arnold on to victory. "Gentleman Johnny" Burgoyne sniffed, when surrendering to "Granny" Gates at Saratoga, "The fortunes of war have made me your prisoner." Actually, it was the misfortunes of Benedict Arnold. When Johnny and Granny sat down together to dine after the ceremony, Arnold lay on a hospital table begging to have his twice-wounded left leg spared from the surgeon's saw. Gates replied to Burgoyne, "I shall always be ready to testify that it [the British defeat] has not been through any fault of your Excellency." Gates's report to Congress and George Washington on the American victory at Saratoga omitted Arnold's action, thus planting in the egotistical Benedict the seed of treason.

Later, after his marriage, court-martial and reprimand in Philadelphia, Arnold accepted Peggy's scheme to abandon the United States as a failed experiment in mob rule. Secret letters to Major Andre set up the deal. Arnold would weaken America's fortress at West Point and remove a link from Washington's watch chain. He'd ensure the Hudson fell into British control, switch sides and receive about £20,000 sterling for his efforts. They felt their plot to end the American rebellion would make Andre a general and Arnold a viceroy! Lippard, however, divined:

> *The Phantom will poison his life…As he presses his wife to his lips, that pale face will glide between, muttering that soundless curse.*
>
> *To escape that Phantom, he will hurry from place to place! Now in the snows of Canada, now amid the palm groves of the Southern Isles, now on ship-board, now on shore—still John Andre's ghost will silently glide by his side.*

Crossing the Hudson, 1780 ink on paper. *Copy of sketch by Major John Andre, from* Harper's Monthly, *April 1876. From the collection of the Highland Studio, Inc., Cold Spring, NY.*

Ichabod Crane, en route to his ill-fated encounter with the Headless Horseman, cringed upon approaching "Andre's tree." Worried Andre's ghost would glide by when the schoolmaster "approached this fearful tree, he began to whistle." The massive tulip tree stood near "Wiley's Swamp" just below the Albany Post Road. The whole place was fraught with "mourning cries and wailings."

The spot where the American Skinners John Paulding, David Williams and Isaac Van Wart captured John Andre is now marked with a monument and a park. Here people sense an invisible presence of the ghost. The frightened schoolmaster in *The Legend*, nevertheless, "passed the tree in safety." This took him off guard for the coming encounter with the region's dominant spirit. Andre's spirit, however, is known to haunt in the early morning. Ichabod approached just after "the dead hush of midnight." The Yankee schoolmaster's relief when escaping this Sleepy Hollow specter begs the question: what is "the tragical story of the unfortunate Andre"?

Andre's Journey

The reverberation of cannon fire disrupted a clandestine meeting in the shadows of Long Clove Mountain. "Gustavus" pressed into the hands of "John Anderson" a sheaf of six pages. 'Take these to your superior. They show how to take the American fortress at West Point." Major John Andre objected, "I could be taken as a spy with these on my person." General Arnold scribbled a pass, permitting John Anderson safe passage through all posts to White Plains. Smiling, British major John Andre bid farewell to American general Benedict Arnold. Dashing down the steep Hudson Highland hill, Andre hoped the shots had not come from *The Vulture*.

The British warship *The Vulture* was set off Croton Point to transport Andre after he met and confirmed Arnold's readiness to turn coats. One local legend says a slave and an indentured servant spied the warship and alerted an American colonel, Livingston. Lacking Arnold's approval, Livingston allowed the militia to haul a cannon down to the point. The locals fired, forcing the ship to withdraw from Dobbs Ferry without Andre.

Fate then doomed Andre. Joshua Hett Smith, Andre's local Loyalist guide, convinced the British major to take another course back to New York City. "You are a target in your Redcoat uniform," Smith noted while getting the major to don a disguise of a round beaver felt cap and claret cloak. Smith and his servant rowed John Anderson across the Hudson to Verplanck. Against orders, he carried enemy papers, incognito, into a no-man's land.

Wending his way south through the no-man's land of Upper Westchester, Major John Andre, adjutant general to Sir Henry Clinton, commander in chief of King George's Third's Expeditionary Force in North America, anxiously sought Dobbs Ferry. Andre and Smith spent a fretful night at the home of Andreas Miller, near Pines Bridge (Yorktown Heights). Following a couple of close encounters with wary American officers, Smith abandoned Andre, leaving the Englishman to find his way in a county with signs reading, "Dish his di Roode toe de Kshing's Farry."

The sentry at Pines Bridge, the boundary between British lower and American upper Westchester, warned, "Take heed of the Cow-Boys down there." Andre agreed, showing his pass from Arnold, but he hoped he'd find one of those Loyalist bands driving stolen cattle to British troops in New York City. He forgot about the Patriot Skinners out to make them stop.

He broke fast with a bowl of mush given to him by a Dutch woman at the Underhill House. Evidently, he also accepted a peach from a child near a well. Several miles later, his horse clattered over the little bridge by the Old Dutch Church in Sleepy Hollow. Glimpsing through autumn-tinged trees the expansive Tappan Zee, Andre took heart. Dobbs Ferry was near! A band of Skinners, however, alerted nearby too.

The one clad in a red and green coat he swiped to escape from a Hessian guard stepped forward, aiming a musket. Two other Skinners in plain hunter's frocks hid in the brush, while a handful of others played cards in the next field. They spied a horseman in a common round beaver cap and cloak with military trimmed boots. Relieved to see the coat of a Hessian ally, Major Andre called out, "I see you are with our party!"

The one in the Hessian coat, John Paulding, replied, "What party are you from?"

Andre again considered the gunman's clothes and believed he had finally landed in helping hands. He answered Paulding, "The lower party!"

Paulding gave a quick nod to his compatriots, Isaac van Wart and David Williams, and told the rider they were all with the lower party too.

"Thank God!" Andre gushed. "I am a British officer on particular business in this country and cannot be detained. I must get to General Clinton! Here, let me prove it to you."

The rider produced a fine pocket watch, indicative of his status. "Now, I warn you. Do not detain me for one more minute."

Paulding gave another subtle signal to his compatriots. They stepped up next to the rider. One shot a hand onto the horse's bridle. The other went for the stirrup. Paulding ordered, "Climb down off your mount. We are American Patriots!"

They slipped the rider off his mount. He waved them off and, as Paulding would later testify, "seemed to make a kind of laugh." Finding himself in a pickle, Andre smiled.

"My God, a man must do anything to get along!"

Again, he reached into his pocket, producing for the Skinners a letter. He continued, "I am John Anderson, on a vital errand for General Benedict Arnold. See? I have a pass signed in his own hand." Assuming these "bosslopers" could not read, he pointed to the signature.

Intrigued by the gold watch, they led him off the road and down through the brush to a stream running by a great tulip tree. The trio searched "Anderson's" pockets. They ordered him to remove his waistcoat, cravat, chemise and knee breeches. "Now the boots!"

When the fruitless search exasperated everyone involved, Van Wart exclaimed he felt something in the bottom of the stockings. Paulding pulled them off and discovered a sheaf of folded papers.

"I told you, those pertain to particular business with General Arnold, now please do not detain me any longer!"

Major Andre believed these bumpkins could not read. He was two-thirds right. Paulding deciphered the documents. Recognizing a plan for an attack on West Point, he announced, "This man is a spy!"

Andre insisted he was John Anderson, a merchant. He had received the documents from a man at Pines Bridge. Under protection from Arnold, he had to deliver the papers to Dobbs Ferry.

Van Wart asked, "What will you give us to let you go? How about your horse, saddle and watch?"

"And a hundred guineas!" added Williams.

Andre hastily agreed, explaining he'd direct them to his contact in Kingsbridge, where they could go to collect the money.

"Kingsbridge! That'll bring Redcoats to get us! I thought you said you were with the Americans!"

Paulding then leaped up: "We won't let you go for ten thousand guineas!"

They pinioned their prisoner's arms behind his back, tied him, set him on the horse and called out to their card-playing sergeant, John Dean. They escorted John Anderson to nearby Reed's Tavern, where Old Saw Mill Road now crosses the Saw Mill River Parkway. There the tavern keeper gave them

Andre's capture place, circa 1820. Historical Collections of the State of New York *by John W. Barber and Henry Howe (1842). From the collection of the Highland Studio, Inc., Cold Spring, NY.*

some bread and milk. The Skinners decided to take their captive to an American outpost at Wright's Mill near Armonk. Andre broke into a cold sweat. Despairing, the prisoner blurted, "I would to God you had blown my brains out when you stopped me!"

ANDRE'S CAPTURE

They found a friend of Benedict Arnold's, Lieutenant Colonel John Jameson, on duty. He listened to the trio's story and, at length, to John Anderson's version. The papers clearly showed plans for an attack on West Point. Jameson believed he had found "a plot to ruin Arnold." Misled by Andre's Anderson act, Jameson sent his distinguished prisoner under escort to Benedict Arnold's headquarters at the Robinson House, across from West Point in Garrison! The confused officer also dispatched a lone horse and rider with the papers found on Andre by the Skinners to George Washington, known to be traveling near Danbury, Connecticut.

Later, at night, Major Benjamin Tallmadge, General Washington's spymaster, arrived at Wright's Mill. Jameson reported the "Anderson" incident. Tallmadge, aware of earlier British attempts to turn coats and conscious of Arnold's contempt for Congress, sniffed out a conspiracy. Angered at both Jameson and the trio, who he believed were just ransom seekers, Tallmadge dispatched two messengers. One would intercept the party with Andre. The other would reach Washington with shocking news: "Major General Benedict Arnold is a traitor! We caught his collaborator, a British agent, with plans to weaken West Point for a British take over."

The determined messenger, in a ride rivaling Paul Revere's, intercepted the Andre contingent just a half dozen miles from the safety of Arnold's headquarters at the Robinson House. Tallmadge ordered his soldiers to take Andre to the isolated Gilbert House in present-day South Salem. He wanted his prisoner far from trolling Cow-Boys, Loyalist Rangers and Redcoats. The messenger seeking Washington missed the general's party when they decided to travel via Fishkill Road to the north.

Andre continued to insist he was John Anderson, a merchant tricked into doing Arnold's dirty work. Tallmadge, as spymaster, rode to the Gilbert House to interview this "merchant." Tallmadge observed Andre's military-style boots, powdered hair and refined gait. "As soon as I saw Anderson," Tallmadge noted, "especially after I saw him walk across the floor, I became impressed with the belief that he had been bred to bear arms."

Children gathered in the Gilbert House, wondering why the stranger looked melancholy. They apparently moved this man haunted by guilt to drop his false identity. Writing as Major John Andre, adjutant general, he crafted a rambling letter to his Excellency General George Washington. Mixing regret with hubris, Andre declared Benedict Arnold had deceived him. Acting as Arnold's messenger, circumstance made Andre appear as a spy! What's more, the brash major pointedly declared himself a very prominent person who'd fetch a high price from the British command. Treat me well, Andre warned, or American prisoners will suffer.

Tallmadge ordered escorted Andre over the lonely roads of Upper Westchester and what's now Putnam County. They'd ferry him across the Hudson from Garrison's Landing for a safe trial in Tappan. Near Ma-ho-pac, while resting at the home of James Cox, Andre gazed into a cradle at his host's daughter. The baby blessed the doomed man with a smile. Touched, the British officer cooed, "Happy childhood! We know its peace but once."

Andre made several sketches along the way. One shows Joshua Hett Smith rowing him across the Hudson following his clandestine meeting at Long Clove Mountain with Benedict Arnold. Another, a self-portrait, reveals a doomed man, haunted by the twists his fate had taken.

Arnold's Pawn

When the doomed Major Andre arrived at West Point headquarters in Garrison in the Highlands, wily Arnold, the hero of Quebec, Valcour Island and especially Saratoga, had already escaped. Earlier, on the morning of September 25, Tallmadge's messenger from South Salem had arrived at Robinson House. He gave Arnold the letter of Andre's capture. Slipping into cool Benedict for the aides present, the careful conspirator quipped about the call of duty and slipped off. Gripping his wife, Peggy, in the drawing room, he gave the dreaded news. "They have Andre!" Scribbling a note to Washington exonerating his wife and aides, Arnold took flight.

Commandeering a military boat to travel downriver, Arnold waved a white truce flag to *The Vulture* still anchored off Dobbs Ferry. Upon boarding, he received about £20,000 sterling and a brigadier general's star and became a traitor to the cause he once loved.

Benedict Arnold failed to show up at his headquarters in Garrison to meet his commander in chief. This gave George Washington "vague misgivings." The commander in chief then inspected the fortifications and discovered them in rough shape. Washington then received shocking news. The messenger arrived with evidence of Arnold's plot to give the British West Point. General Washington, before his junior officers, appeared to take the news of the betrayal rather calmly. Next he steadfastly faced a hysterical Peggy performing histrionics to buy her husband more time to escape. Washington ordered Alexander Hamilton to ride with a couple of men to intercept Arnold. They were too late.

Later over dinner, Washington confided to his trusted officers, Alexander Hamilton, Henry Knox and the Marquis de Lafayette, "Arnold is a traitor flown now to the British. Whom now can we trust?" Tears streamed down the commander in chief's cheeks.

Fourteen American generals sat to judge the strange case of Major John Andre. During the proceedings, Andre remained captive in the Mabie House (now the Old 76 House) in Tappan, New York. Many of the younger officers, Hamilton and Lafayette among them, fell under Andre's charming melancholy spell. They pleaded for an exchange, arguing that the honorable Andre had fallen into Arnold's trap. Washington agreed to an exchange but only for betraying Benedict.

General Sir Henry Clinton also appreciated his aide-de-camp's charm and honorable service. Benedict Arnold, however, was now his grand prize.

Self-portrait, October 1, 1780, ink on paper. *By Major John Andre. Yale University Art Gallery, Gift of Ebenezer Baldwin, B.A., 1808.*

Clinton knew his superiors in England wanted to keep this catch at all costs. Alas, for poor Andre, there would be no trade, just a hanging.

George Washington informally asked the tribunal, chaired by the steely General Nathanael Greene, to be mindful of the British treatment of Captain Nathan Hale. Caught spying in the guise of schoolmaster, the twenty-one-year-old Patriot received no trial. The day after his capture, near Dove's Tavern in New York City, Hale suffered the hangman's noose. Washington, to be sure, avoided the beguiling British officer now gallantly facing the gallows for Arnold's crime.

The American tribunal permitted Andre's artful proclamation of innocence. His complicity, he stated, came while doing his duty. "I had been made into Arnold's pawn!" The tribunal accepted this. Nevertheless, they determined Major John Andre, caught out of uniform with incriminating papers, was a spy. Therefore he shall hang.

"I Am Not to Die on a Gibbet"

John Andre loathed the method of execution. He wrote to Washington, begging, "I am not to die on a gibbet." Still, he accepted his fate manfully. He bravely told visitors, from his own orderly to Alexander Hamilton, to remain composed or step outside to avoid a shameful show of emotion.

When his final day came on October 2, 1780, a ballad of the day would later lament that John Andre "looked both meek and mild." When Colonel Alexander Scammel, the officer in charge, demurely asked his prisoner, "Are you ready?" Andre, once again in his splendid scarlet uniform, answered with a hint of hubris, "Certainly, Colonel."

Two American captains arrived at the Mabie House to usher this unique prisoner to the execution grounds at Old Tappan, New Jersey. Hundreds thronged the road to witness Major John Andre's death. General John Glover noted an odd smile parting Andre's lips as his two escorts locked arms to walk him to the gallows. Giving nods and courtly bows to the gathered generals from his tribunal, even taking Major Benjamin Tallmadge's hand, Andre moved the crowd to tears. He blanched before the sight of the gallows, wondering, "Must I die this way?"

Before mounting the gallows platform, Andre answered his own question in a bold voice. "It will be but a momentary pang." He doffed his hat and placed it on his coffin. A witness observed Andre "had long beautiful hair which agreeable to fashion was wound with a black cloth and hung down his back."

Scammel asked if he had anything to say. Andre took a few deliberate steps forward. He stated: "I have nothing more than this. That I would have you gentlemen bear me witness that I die a brave man."

Smeared with black grease, the executioner, an anxious Cow-Boy named Strickland from the notorious Claudius Smith gang, nervously shook the noose. Muttering to keep his black hands off, Andre swiped the rope from the man. He put it around his own neck, adjusting it behind the right ear to make for a clean job. Andre produced the handkerchiefs needed to secure his arms and cover his eyes.

Some say Andre found his fate through his own succession of errors. Others argued he was a victim of Arnold's guile. His journey to the gallows may have been thwarted if he had but taken other steps. Pointedly, Andre did not shake hands with any of his three captors. What options could have flashed through his mind in this moment before death? "Why didn't I just show them my pass from Arnold?" "Why did I not push by those Skinners?"

"Why did I agree to take Arnold's plans?" "Why did I remove my uniform?" "Will they remember me with kindness?" "Hang Benedict Arnold!" Alas, we shall never know.

The muffled drums rolled. Strickland found enough courage to shimmy up the gallows pole to set the other end of Andre's noose. The crowd wailed and cried, "For pity sake, no!" Would Washington ride in with a pardon? He pointedly stayed away.

Scammel lowered his sword; Strickland took the order. He cracked a whip over the two horses attached to the execution cart. They pulled out the support under Andre's feet. The rope gave a "tremendous swing." A profound stillness quieted the crowd.

A tearful Major Tallmadge, along with all those witnessing Andre's death, felt that "when I saw him swinging under the gibbet, it seemed for a time as if I could not support it." Old Tallmadge admitted years later he could not read an account of poor Andre "without shedding tears of sorrow."

Dr. James Thatcher noted in his extensive journal, "The spot was consecrated with tears by the thousands…Could Arnold have been suspended on the gibbet erected for Andre, not a tear or a sigh would have been produced, but exultation and joy would have been visible on every countenance"

INTERMENT

Major John Andre's body was cut down and viewed by a weeping mob. Scammel saw to the burial detail, while Tallmadge, Alexander Hamilton and the Marquis de Lafayette attended. They marked their companion in arms' grave with only a stack of stones. A tombstone would be an affront to the new nation.

A strange woman in a calico dress, with loose hair and herbs under her apron strings, however, appeared to leave a kind of memorial. She planted a peach pit over the grave. But a local tale claims the peach came from another source. A few miles from Sleepy Hollow, Andre, feeling safe, had paused at the home of Staats Hammond, a Quaker from Chappaqua. His son, David, and daughter, Sally, gawked at the handsome visitor in a cap, cloak and fine military boots. Andre asked for a cup of well water. Sally obliged. Grateful, Andre smiled and gave her a sixpence. Feeling perhaps overcompensated, Sally gave the gentleman a peach. Some believe Andre carried its pit with him to the execution as a reminder of the small act of kindness.

The unfortunate death of Major Andre, 1783 copy of engraving. *By John Goldar, National Archives, College Park, Maryland.*

Forty years later, Great Britain sent a fine vessel, the *Phaeton*, with a stately sarcophagus to collect the compatriot's remains. A large group of locals gathered, emoting for "poor Andre" and fretting that the grave had been robbed. When the British contingent appeared for a tour of "Andre's prison room" at Mabie's Tavern, locals took drinks and warning: "Any display of affection for Andre would insult the memory of George Washington." Still they carefully exhumed the body with some ceremony and plenty of clamor. They found all the bones intact, ready for a proper reinterment at Westminster Abbey in London. Curiously, the roots from a peach tree completely engulfed the skull.

ANDRE'S TREE

Another hero's marker stands on the battlefield in Saratoga. It's a peculiar statue of a boot on a stone pedestal, with the inscription: "In memory of the most brilliant soldier of the Continental army, who was desperately wounded on this spot, winning for his countrymen the decisive battle of the American Revolution, and for himself the rank of Major General."

The tribute acknowledges the extraordinary service of Benedict Arnold. People around Sleepy Hollow, however, held only the memory of Arnold's betrayal. Fighting for the British, Arnold won battles at Richmond, Virginia, and New London, Connecticut, but he never received the trust and respect he craved. He tried to succeed in the military, in trade and land speculation. Arnold's efforts ended with lawsuits, duels and financial losses. He died in England of dropsy in June 1801.

When word of Arnold's death reached the lower Hudson Valley, cheers broke forth wildly. Patrons poured out of Van Tassel's tavern and ran whooping down the Post Road in a race to ring the Old Dutch Church in celebration of the news.

The skies suddenly filled with dark clouds. The moment the Sleepy Hollow gang rang the bell, the spirits seemed to respond in kind. A solitary jolt of lightning shot down and struck off a branch from an ancient tulip tree. The limb fell from the tree where Andre was captured twenty years earlier. Huzzah, they cried, all for the death of Arnold. They then gave a louder cheer for poor John Andre.

"What Party Are You From?"

Cheers for Andre in the dawning nineteenth century gave rise to reports of his ghostly presence near the "Capture Spot" beneath the old tulip tree. Occasionally, early morning travelers along Andre's route on Old Albany Post Road in the Sleepy Hollow detected the sound of muffled hooves of a rider at a hurried pace. The slower travelers move right to let the faster rider pass them by. They hear the approaching horse whinny. The rider gasps frightfully and dashes by unseen. An unearthly chill clings to the air and bodies as Andre's ghost passes. The real horror, however, follows. A piteous wailing, or as Washington Irving describes it "a doleful lamentation," emanates from around a stream known as Andre's Brook. This is the place where the Skinners stripped Andre to find the incriminating plans for West Point. The forlorn spirit tries again to slip by the Skinners to avoid the noose. Thus he moans and shrieks. A few declare Andre's ghost wails, "Why did they hang me and not Arnold?"

By midcentury, when the train began hauling milk to New York City, dairymen learned how to spare themselves the cries Andre dared not utter at his execution. They agreed on the way to stop Andre's spirit from uttering his lamentation. One must use the words Skinner John Paulding used to catch the disguised British major, calling out, "What party are you from?" This phrase silences Andre's spirit. The icy sensation then dissipates, though some insist a faint scent of peach lingers in the air as the ghost vanishes.

An air of controversy surrounding Major John Andre's fate remains to this day in Sleepy Hollow and environs. It took local people decades before

Tulip tree at Andre's capture place, 2009, Tarrytown/Sleepy Hollow, New York. *Photo by Todd Atteberry, www.thehistorytrekker.com.*

agreeing to raise a monument. It acknowledges not only his captors but Andre too. Was Andre an imprudent victim of Benedict Arnold's conspiracy or a determined British Loyalist? Apparently, only his ghost knows the answer.

Chapter 7

BALT, BROM, KATRINA
AND ICHABOD

It is with infinite difficulty I have been enabled to collect these biographical
anecdotes.
—Diedrich Knickerbocker

The difficulties Washington Irving's storytelling alter ego faced when writing his *History of New-York* apply to the task of unearthing the real Headless Horseman of Sleepy Hollow and his ghostly cohorts. Collecting the goods on *The Legend's* iconic characters of Balt, Brom, Katrina and Ichabod poses another challenge. Irving played fast and loose with fact and fiction when caricaturing the Dutch people he adored. Carl Carmer, in his definitive 1939 book *The Hudson*, felt the need to redefine Dutch New Netherlanders as "hard, blond traders" rather than "the fatheaded, fat-bottomed, sleepy sillily pompous folk of the Knickerbocker History." Nevertheless, *The Legend's* coquettish Katrina, roistering Brom, snug Balt and interloping Ichabod emerged from actual individuals living around 1800 in the Hudson Valley. Irving the lawyer cleverly guided Irving the writer when establishing these characters. They stand right on the edge of today's common disclaimer: "All characters in this work are purely fictitious. Any resemblance to real persons living or dead is purely coincidental." A verisimilitude to real people exists and animates *The Legend*. Incidentally, Irving's real-life Katrina source didn't mind modeling; neither did the two Broms. One Ichabod proudly showed proof of his role in *The Legend*, while another, some say, took umbrage when Irving used his name.

Today, tourists hoping to find the actual people behind *The Legend*'s characters flock to Sleepy Hollow's Old Dutch Church Cemetery. They point to the headstone of "Catriena van Tessel" and exclaim, "Here's the real Katrina van Tassel!" They don't know she just lent her everyday-sounding name for the story. The real source lies under the marker for Eleanor van Tassel Bush.

The grave of Abraham Martling puts them about as near as Irving lets anyone get to Abraham "Brom Bones" van Brunt. Next they look for the Headless Horseman's grave. Washington Irving tells us the decapitated Hessian was "buried in the church-yard." This refers to the unmarked potter's field in a northeast corner, where the poor and outcasts like Hulda the Witch would have been interred. Curiosity inexorably moves people to want to separate the facts on Balt, Brom, Katrina and Ichabod from Irving's fiction. A look at the names used in *The Legend of Sleepy Hollow* helps in this quest.

BALT

*Old Baltus Van Tassel was a perfect picture of a thriving, contented, liberal-hearted farmer. He seldom it is true sent either of his eyes of thoughts beyond the boundaries of his own farm; but within those everything was snug, happy, and well-conditioned. He was satisfied with his wealth, but not proud of it (*TLSH, 22).

Irving employs the moniker Baltus van Tassel to portray a farmer well off but down to earth. Seventeenth-century Dutch merchants celebrated lucrative trade at Baltic Sea ports by naming sons "Baltus." It was rather like calling your son "Washington" right after the American Revolution. Both names reflect the values of their times. Balts were rich guys. The surname Van Tassel, however, tempers the bounty associated with Baltus. A common name even today in the Hudson Valley, Van Tassel means "of Tessel," an isolated island in the Netherlands. So, Baltus and Katrina are at once wealthy and quaint.

When seeking the original Baltus van Tassel farm, many just look across the road from the Old Dutch Church. There stands the venerable Philipse family's manor house. Washington Irving's obituary sites Philipseburg Manor as the model for Van Tassel's house in *The Legend*. Frederick Philipse owned over fifty thousand acres of land in Westchester. Cultivation by hundreds of tenant farmers, indentured servants and slaves made Philipse the richest man in the colonies at the time of the Revolution. Certainly his manor proffered the mouth-watering bounty coveted by Ichabod.

Old Balt, on the other hand, owned "a vast barn, that might have served for a church; every window and crevice of which seemed bursting forth with the treasures of the farm." Frederick's treasure did fill many a sloop on the Hudson for trade around the world. Philipse, then, was no mere Van Tassel.

Henry Steiner, in *The Place Names of Historic Sleepy Hollow*, suggests another source for Van Tassel's farm: "It seems that Washington Irving never wrote about Castle Philipse and its mill (though he mentions the mill fleetingly). The description of Baltus van Tassel's farm in *The Legend of Sleepy Hollow* might well have been based on his Castle in the post-Revolutionary days of the Beekman ownership."

Philipse profited immensely with a king ruling the colonies. His ten-room place on the Pocantico served primarily as his office and shipping depot. His primary residence was a thirty-plus-room mansion in Yonkers. A staunch Loyalist, he fled to England soon after the Revolutionary War broke out. Later when Philipse's huge estate was divided up to help pay for the war, a prosperous Patriot named Beekman took over a smaller portion of the manor. Still, Beekman's estate remained grander than Baltus van Tassel's farm.

Some folks from Croton on Hudson, about ten miles north of Sleepy Hollow, proclaim Van Cortlandt Manor as the site for Van Tassel's farm. Again, it is a large manor, not a respectable Dutch "bouwery." The local references given in Ichabod's famed race with the Headless Horseman to the Old Dutch Church Bridge don't lead to Van Cortlandt's as the Van Tassel place.

The thriving farms around Tarrytown, a place named for the Dutch "tarwe," or wheat, impressed Washington Irving. Yet no single place stands out in Westchester as the model for Balt's farm. Finding Balt's farm requires a look about 120 miles north of Sleepy Hollow. There, among the abundant fields, bright orchards and overstocked ponds of old Columbia County, New York, appears the Van Tassel bouwery.

A heartbroken Washington Irving found the farm that would become Van Tassel's when he visited Kinderhook. There a dear friend, William van Ness, took in the devastated lawyer/writer. Irving's beloved Matilda Hoffman, a dark-eyed frail beauty, died of yellow fever in April 1809. His father and sister also passed away early that winter. Irving, to escape his woe, toured about the upper Hudson Valley. He noticed the sturdy high-roofed home with ample surrounding farmland of the 1734 Luycas van Alen homestead. It echoed some features found in a homestead owned by a blacksmith in Sleepy Hollow named Abraham Matlengh (later anglicized to Martling). Built in 1730, the stone farmhouse stood farther down what's now Beekman Road, a couple miles west of Philipseburg Manor on the Hudson. "His [Van Tassel's] stronghold was situated on the banks of the Hudson." Martling's house offered a gracious "stoep," double Dutch doors, broad porches and all the accoutrements Washington Irving describes in a grand old Dutch "bouwery" on the Hudson: "It was one of those spacious farmhouses, with high-ridged but lowly sloping roofs, built in the style handed down from the first Dutch settlers; the low projecting eaves forming a piazza along the front, capable of being closed up in bad weather" (*TLSH*, 25).

The Martling house first enchanted the traveling teen Irving during his Sleepy Hollow visits. The Van Alen farm impressed the vulnerable, mourning Irving in 1809. The Sleepy Hollow and Kinderhook houses provided the sensibility for *The Legend*'s Van Tassel house. But another piece in the Van Tassel estate puzzle remains on the table.

THE GOBLIN RACE

Racing a goblin from the Philipse/Beekman place to the Old Dutch Church only requires a crossing of the Albany Post Road. This manor house stands too close for a real flight from a galloping specter. Clues found in the geography noted in *The Legend* help locate the original Van Tassel house. Ichabod discerns a dog barking across the Hudson, placing the estate on the southeast shore of the Tappan Zee, below today's Governor Malcolm Wilson Bridge.

> *Ichabod…pursued his travel homewards, along the sides of the lofty hills which rise above Tarry Town, and which he had traversed so cheerily in the afternoon. The hour was dismal as himself. Far below him, the Tappan Zee spread its dusky and indistinct waste of waters, with here and there the tall mast of a sloop, riding quietly at anchor under the land. In the dead hush of midnight, he could even hear the barking of the watch dog from the opposite shore of the Hudson; but it was so vague and faint as only to give an idea of his distance from this faithful companion of man (*TLSH, 58*).*

The dismal schoolmaster embarks on his odyssey within earshot of the west Hudson's west bank. Note that the river expands to over three miles at the north end of the Tappan Zee near Van Cortlandt's at Croton on Hudson. It's almost as wide at Philipse's in Sleepy Hollow. It'd be tough to hear a hound from either of these locales even on a still night. The likely point on the west Hudson for the barking is now Piermont, known in Dutch days as Tappan Slote. Ichabod, after his rejection by Katrina, ascends "far above" the river toward the "lofty hills"—now called Tappan Kykuit and Hackley. The most plausible place for Ichabod to set out for his legendary race lies a couple miles south of old "Tarry Town," where the river is not only narrower but also has the vaulting Palisades to carry out sounds.

Ghost stories told the evening of Balt van Tassel's "quilting frolic" carry on to haunt Ichabod. Perched on the ornery Gunpowder, his borrowed horse, the trembling Master Crane clops along a forlorn section of Old Albany Post Road. The superstitious schoolmaster feels nature conspiring to turn trees into goblins and night birds into uncouth ghouls. Nevertheless, they slip unscathed beneath the monstrous branches of Andre's tulip tree, which once stood in today's Patriots Park on the Tarrytown/Sleepy Hollow border. A presence there spooks Gunpowder into dragging the pedagogue kicking and screaming off course into the haunts of Wiley's Swamp. Today this neighborhood bustles about Valley and Wildey Streets.

Encountering a cloaked headless traveler, Gunpowder takes a "plunge to the opposite side of the road." The only real road there then was the Albany Post. Bolting, Ichabod's one-eyed mare misses the uphill "road which turns off to Sleepy Hollow." Today it's called Bedford Road. Gunpowder flees to "the left," taking a sandy, shady hollow now called Gory Brook Road. Crane hopes for safety. "If I can but reach that bridge," which over two hundred years ago spanned the Pocantico, a long football pass east of the Old Dutch Church. The Headless Horseman, as Brom Bones foretold in his ghost race tale, cannot cross that bridge. Alas, while traversing that wooden bridgework, poor Ichabod gets brained.

Crane's race makes Wolfert's Roost the most likely location for *The Legend*'s Van Tassel house. Roost is an English corruption of the Dutch word "roest," meaning rust. A respectable homestead established in 1656 by Wolfert Eckert, it became in the 1760s the esteemed Jacob van Tassel's farmhouse. Later the place enchanted the rambling young Washington Irving. Returning to the region in 1835, Irving, the world's most successful writer at the time, purchased the old estate and renamed it Sunnyside. The spell of this ancient Dutch bouwery compelled Irving to buy the place and most probably swayed him to make it the setting of *The Legend*.

Three early Dutch farmhouses compose the imagined estate of Baltus van Tassel. Apparently enough snug Dutch landowners endured throughout the region to make it possible for Irving to create Balt without any one model. Building an old-fashioned house may have been a pragmatic choice handed down by Dutch fathers to sons. Firth Haring Fabend, however, in his book *A Dutch Family in the Middle Colonies*, notes the old-style homes originate in the deep conservatism of the Dutch folk Washington Irving encountered throughout his ramblings in the Hudson Valley:

> *He* [the Dutch American] *was ambivalent about America... Hundreds of sandstone houses built in Bergen and Rockland long after the Revolution—represents his misgivings about America and becoming American. By rejecting America's demand for newness, innovation and change, the Dutch farmer was rejecting the very spirit of progressivism that impelled him to America. But in doing so he is rejecting all the violence that newness, innovation and change had wreaked upon an older ideal that had ended by dividing and damaging his family, church and community.*

Dutch ways persisted long after Peter Stuyvesant peacefully surrendered the New Netherlands to the English in 1664. People of the Hudson Valley spoke Dutch while keeping their Old World customs and cookery well into the early nineteenth century. Martlenghs and Van Alen clearly followed Dutch homebuilding traditions.

The provincial Baltus, "without a thought beyond his farm and daughter's marriage," indeed rejects the violence of American change. He'd never accept a Connecticut Yankee schoolmaster as a son-in-law. Plus, Balt remains unperturbed, puffing his pipe, "watching the achievements of a little wooden warrior," when Ichabod courts Katrina. Baltus van Tassel sits as a stalwart against the migrating tides of change coming along the Hudson. Irving took refuge in a Balt-like home when a wandering teen and later when a melancholy young man.

Any world-weary traveler would welcome an invitation to this good-natured fellow's "quilting frolic." What joy "to help yourself and fall to it" at Balt's bountiful table! Following the hearty meal and a lively dance, folks roast apples, puff long-stemmed pipes and listen to a few ghost stories. Soon all heartache and haste dissipate around the Dutch hearth:

I mention this peaceful spot with all possible laud for it is in such little retired Dutch valleys, found here and there embosomed in the great State of New York, that population, manners, and customs remain fixed, while the great torrent of migration and improvement, which is making such incessant changes in other parts of this restless country, sweeps by them unobserved (TLSH, 8).

Again, Balt rises not from any one man Irving met in an isolated Dutch hollow. He's the steadfast folk under the Dutch spell, holding out in the Hudson Valley.

Another figure roars out of the Hudson Valley. Irving got to know in Kinderhook one Abraham (Brom) van Alstyn. A brawny blacksmith, he gave Irving inspiration to create the Herculean Brom Bones. He, like Balt, embodies the manners and ways of a traditional Dutchman. This "rollicking roystering blade," made of "more mischief than malice," however, is a unique American character.

BROM

He was famed for great knowledge and skill in horsemanship, being as dexterous on horseback as a Tartar. He was foremost at all races and cock fights; and, with the ascendancy which bodily strength always acquires in rustic life, was the umpire in all disputes, setting his hat on one side, and giving his decisions with an air and tone that admitted of no gainsay or appeal. He was always ready for either a fight or a frolic; but had more mischief than ill will in his composition; and with all his overbearing roughness, there was a strong dash of waggish good humor at bottom (TLSH, 28).

Abraham van Brunt rides into our consciousness, making an indelible dark impression in the guise of a galloping goblin. Granted, Diedrich Knickerbocker's storyteller never plainly states Brom Bones is the Headless Horseman of Sleepy Hollow. *The Legend's* teller strongly suggests Brom just dressed up like the ghost: "[Brom] always burst into a hearty laugh at the mention of the pumpkin; which led some to suspect that he knew more about the matter than he chose to tell" (*TLSH*, 72).

If Brom chased off Ichabod, are skeptics right to assert that there is no actual Headless Horseman of Sleepy Hollow? *The Legend's* storyteller counters, "The old country wives, who are the best judges" of these spooky matters, know the ghost of a galloping Hessian still creates midnight blasts while scouring the countryside for his head.

Indeed, in the late nineteenth century, renowned folklorist Edgar Mayhew Bacon heard a story of an encounter with the Headless Horseman from an Irish washerwoman. Impatient over her husband's tarrying at Van Tassel's tavern, a noise outside moved the woman to creak open the top of her cottage's double Dutch door. She leaned out into the chilling night air. Mounted on a sparking horse, a monstrous goblin rose up with a head in his hand. The petrified woman barely managed to slam shut the door before the ghoul hurled that projectile at the snooping woman. When Bacon tried to dismiss her story as evidence of Irving's life imitating art, the woman invited the skeptic to come see the Horseman's bloody stain on her door! The Friends of the Old Dutch Church still collect Headless Horseman sightings today. Clearly, the spirit of the galloping headless Hessian rides beyond Brom Bones.

Scholars and storytellers from Columbia and Westchester Counties champion their respective Abrahams—Van Alstyn and Martling—as Brom Bones. Another historian cites an Abraham van Tassel. All are crafty blacksmiths. One, however, stands out as the model for *The Legend*'s Abraham van Brunt. The old veterans at the Van Tassel frolic share their Revolutionary War stories after Ichabod's frenetic dance with Katrina. "Doffue" Martling boasts that he fought off the British fleet in the Tappan Zee with a six-pound cannon. An actual veteran, this Captain Daniel Martling fought honorably in many local skirmishes. Daniel's relative, Abraham (grandson of the Martlenghs who built the 1730 Sleepy Hollow on the Hudson House), also demonstrated some clever heroics. When the Patriot Van Tassel cousins, Peter and Cornelius, suffered the destruction of their farms near Elmsford, militiamen elected blacksmith Abraham Martling as raid captain to lead a retaliatory attack on the home of Loyalist leader Oliver DeLancey. Captain Martling guided his men down the Hudson with muffled oars. They slipped by Loyalist guards to burn DeLancey's house. Both bold and cunning, this "Brom" demonstrated the character found later in Irving's Brom. Thus, Abraham Martling shows the mix of mischief with a lesser dose of malice needed to win the Revolution. No doubt Abraham van Brunt is composed of a few real blacksmiths named Abraham. The Dutch Brom Bones foreshadows the coming of other blunt and brawny, wild and wily American characters.

Bold Brom, of course, cunningly spooked away Ichabod in order to escort Katrina to the altar at the Old Dutch Church. How could Katrina resist

Brom Bones and Pumpkin Head, 1893 illustration. *By George Boughton for* Rip Van Winkle *and* The Legend of Sleepy Hollow *by Washington Irving*

"his over-bearing roughness" tempered by his "strong dash of waggish good humor"? His method has roots in ancient European and Dutch customs carried on in the New World. Brom practiced an old trick in using a disguise to frighten off a rival.

KATRINA

Could that girl have been playing off any of her coquettish tricks? Was her encouragement of the poor pedagogue all a mere sham to secure her conquest of his rival? Heaven only knows, not I!

Katrina van Tassel stepped out into the American landscape from a tradition of independent Dutch women. A colonial English woman was her husband's "femme posse," or female possession. If widowed, an English woman's inheritance had to be managed by her closest male relative. New

Netherland laws (which the Dutch were allowed to keep after English takeover of the colony in 1664) gave men and women mutual wills. Indeed, the Philipse family became rich in part because Frederick married Margaret Hardenbroeck, a Dutch widow who had inherited her own fortune.

Young, independent, flirtatious coquettes no doubt beguiled Washington Irving up and down the Hudson Valley. Up in Columbia County, they make a strong case for Helena van Alen as Katrina's inspiration. A beauty, as feisty as Matilda Hoffman was fay, Helena certainly charmed Irving. The vivacious Eleanor van Tassel, however, really gave Irving his Katrina. Daughter of the fighting American Patriot Jacob, she became the object of a raid during the war. Loyalist Cow-Boys attacked the Van Tassel farm, the old Wolfert's Roost. They took cattle, set the house on fire and couldn't resist carrying off the budding Eleanor. Cursing and kicking, she hollered for help. The equally spirited Van Tassel women, in true Dutch form, took charge of the situation. They clobbered the Cow-Boys to rescue their "Laney."

The innumerable Van Tassel clan had spread throughout Hudson Valley by the early 1800s. Eleanor's family dwelled at Wolfert's Roost when young Washington hunted nearby. She lived in Sleepy Hollow for her entire long life, into her nineties, and no doubt knew Washington Irving. His sister boarded at the Van Tassel family tavern. Granted, the gravestone for Catriena van Tassel taken on face value seems to say she is *The Legend*'s Katrina. This Catriena was over a decade older than Laney van Tassel and not noted for her high spirits. Names matter to Washington Irving. He selected two very popular monikers, Katrina and Van Tassel, for his heroine. Thus, Irving puts forth her character as the quintessential young Dutch woman of the Hudson Valley.

The Legend's Katrina never kicks or curses; she dances with the kinetic Ichabod Crane, accepting all his "ooglings" just to make Brom jealous. Is she duplicitous or just plain clever? She could not bear Brom's courtship practices, which "consist[ed] of a lot of pawing." She expected something else from him: a marriage proposal. Ichabod misread her intentions at the quilting frolic. If the Yankee schoolmaster had been aware of the local Dutch courtship customs, he would have known Katrina's intention earlier. When a Dutch woman lets a man come calling, she indicates her level of interest by providing her suitor with a pipe. The fancier the pipe, the more she fancies him! The only pipe fetched for psalm-master Ichabod was the pitch pipe. Katrina, like all the countrywomen, finds the odd pedagogue charming but doesn't take him seriously. Her father, of course, took comfort in his daughter's wiles, leaving Balt to puff, worry free, on his own pipe.

ICHABOD

The cognomen of Crane was not inapplicable to his person. He was tall, but exceedingly lank, with narrow shoulders, long arms and legs, hands that dangled a mile out of his sleeves, feet that might have served for shovels, and his whole frame most loosely hung together. His head was small, and flat at top, with huge ears, large green glassy eyes, and a long snipe nose, so that it looked like a weathercock perched upon his spindle neck to tell which way the wind blew. To see him striding along the profile of a hill on a windy day, with his clothes bagging and fluttering about him, one might have mistaken him for the genius of famine descending upon the earth, or some scarecrow eloped from a cornfield.

When death took away Maltida Hoffman, all those who knew Washington Irving took pity on him. He lost his beloved, shy fiancée just before her eighteenth birthday. Some see Matilda in Katrina and Irving in Ichabod. The beguiling Miss van Tassel is the sincere Miss Hoffman's complete opposite. Irving often fell for serious, ethereal teen beauties. He set these girls on pedestals to be adored and abandoned. Ichabod adored the beautiful Katrina but salivated the more for the bounty of her father's farm.

One story suggests the real Sleepy Hollow schoolmaster at the time of Irving's visits became the template for Ichabod Crane. Samuel Youngs came from New England like Ichabod. He left the area to study law, winding up, like the fictional schoolmaster, serving in the courts. Youngs, though, was no trembling scarecrow! He fought with distinction during the Revolutionary War.

Another tale of the source for that "worthy wight" schoolmaster comes from Washington Irving's letters. Writing to his friend Sir Walter Scott, with whom he stayed in Abbotsford, the young American author recalled a local teacher he met in Scotland: "That worthy wight Lockie Longlegs, whose appearance I shall never forget striding along the profile of a knoll in his red night cap, with his flimsy garments fluttering about him."

Curiously, the story gains credence since the letter was written while Irving worked on *The Sketchbook* in England. Granted, Lockie looks like Ichabod. There's more to the story of Ichabod than his beaky gangling appearance. An actual account of a chase by a rival in a ghost guise came Irving's way while in Kinderhook.

When three deaths, including Matilda's, threatened to overwhelm Irving, William van Ness invited the mourning writer to Lindenwald, his estate in Kinderhook, Columbia County, New York. The patchwork fields and gentle hills and the Van Alens, the Van Alstynes and other old Dutch families together would heal Irving's broken heart. Further, they'd later provide some inspiration!

Washington Irving at Kinderhook found a tonic for his woe in the Dutch tales he heard there. Tucked away from the changing cities of Albany and New York, Kinderhook stood as one of those isolated Dutch communities where the "customs remained fixed." Indeed, when President Martin van Buren retired there, he fondly recalled chatting with an old woman who told him tales in "Holland, not American Dutch." Kinderhook gave Irving the true core of *The Legend*. Once again, a key tale of Dutch Americans comes from an outsider, a Connecticut Yankee and itinerant schoolmaster named Jesse Merwin.

THE HEADLESS HORSEMAN CHARIVARI OF KINDERHOOK

Merwin had been courting Jane van Dyck, a local Dutch woman, for several years when he fell into a trap set by local custom. Abram van Alstyne, who never expressed any interest in Jane, burst into the schoolhouse to threaten, "Jesse Merwin! Stay away from my lady!" The brawny blacksmith looked ready to teach the teacher a tough lesson.

Later that evening, Merwin went calling on his sweetheart. She offered him something unusual: an ornate tobacco pipe. The schoolmaster still made no offer of marriage. Riding back on a borrowed horse, a peculiar figure silently accosted Merwin. The stranger wore an old soldier's uniform beneath a huge cloak. Imagine Merwin relating his horror when describing to Irving, "My travel companion, had no head!" Next, the headless rider gave an uncouth howl and chased after the schoolmaster. Wailing and raging, the stranger attempted to drive Merwin away. The voice, though unearthly, was familiar. Merwin recognized his said rival, Abram van Alstyne!

Both raced off without exchanging a word. The next day, the scared Merwin went straight to Jane and begged her to marry him.

Brom van Alstyne, of course, brought the biggest smile of all to the wedding. He led the mischief makers in tossing grain against the couple's window on their first night together. He always gave a knowing laugh whenever the subject of Merwin's courtship came up.

Jesse Merwin had been moved to marry by the ancient custom of a charivari. The community often took action when a couple dillydallied or shilly-shallied. Tradition called for friends and family to test the couple's love. They'd either drive the man off or drive him to the altar. This explains Brom van Alstyn's "claim" on Jane, followed by the charivari. Dressing up as a ghost, he hides his identity, covering up the test. The chased man could always claim that a ghost frightened him. He wasn't tricked into marriage! Of course, if the charivari moved the couple to marry, a great celebration followed. It's been documented that Merwin confided the story of his charivari to Washington Irving. It's fair to say Ichabod's wild St. Vitus with Katrina was part of her plan to move Brom into a charivari.

Merwin welcomed the Hudson Valley Dutch variation of a charivari. West of the Mississippi, the tradition known as a "shivaree" served as a way the community acknowledged newlyweds. They'd dress in costumes, often as ghosts, to serenade and blast horns below the couple's window. Nineteenth-century upstate New Yorkers also used the term "horning" when driving a man into or away from a marriage. Here Brom van Alstyne drove his friend Jesse Merwin to Jane van Dyck. A less worthy wight may have just kept on running to suffer the fate of having to become a city lawyer!

JESSE MERWIN, THE REAL SCHOOLMASTER

Sharing the courtship story led to a strong friendship between Merwin and Irving. Later, the estate became famed as Martin van Buren's country retreat. The eighth president boasted that Irving met his Katrina, Brom Bones and, of course, Ichabod while in Kinderhook. Van Buren himself certified in a letter Jesse Merwin as the model for *The Legend of Sleepy Hollow*'s Yankee schoolmaster. Years later, Irving gave his own proof to Merwin. The author addressed a letter to Jesse Merwin as "the original Ichabod Crane."

Jesse Merwin's charming, sparse schoolhouse still stands in Kinderhook, complete with the teacher's initials carved in the wood. The well-preserved Old Van Alen House evokes the setting for a courting schoolmaster and Katrina. The Columbia County Historical Society lists these hallowed places as the inspiration for *The Legend of Sleepy Hollow*. Their claim holds up in the local lore and landscape.

Colonel Ichabod Crane

There lived an actual man named Ichabod Crane. An officer during the War of 1812, Major Ichabod Crane's campaign adventures in Sackets Harbor, New York, though noteworthy, were not exceptionally heroic. His exploits interested Washington Irving enough for a meeting after the war. It provided the author with an onomatopoeia description for

Colonel Ichabod Crane, circa 1857. *Unknown photographer, Photo Lab Archive, Santa Cruz, California.*

a bird-beaked scarecrow of a schoolmaster. Lockie Longlegs alliterates, lopes and looks good on paper, but the name Ichabod Crane sang out for a Yankee pedagogue.

Later, some sources say the real war bird objected vigorously to this appropriation of his moniker. He felt tainted by association with the snipe-nosed teacher. One look at the daguerreotype of an elderly Colonel Crane shows a resemblance in name only. Irving's Ichabod shaped the archetypical, charmingly clueless nerd we love to frighten. He is the geek who goes on to get some revenge on the bullies either as a lawyer or a Sleepy Hollow ghost.

Merwin's Ghost

A relatively recent bit of lore says Jesse Merwin and his wife, Jane, still "dwell" around their former home. A retired actress from New York City bought the place as a summer retreat. She made some repairs and gave the farmhouse a coat of paint but kept everything as it was—save for one thing. Curiosity moved the former thespian to turn over a couple of garden steppingstones made of old grave markers. She hoped to read their inscriptions, but they were too worn.

A fierce storm that night knocked down two maple trees on her property. Local folk say the actress learned the markers belonged to Jesse and his wife. Their spirits, apparently, do not take kindly to being disturbed!

Final Word

Scholar Daniel G. Hoffman tells why the schoolmaster earned the charivari-style drive off from Baltus van Tassel's farm and daughter Katrina: "Brom Bones stays in the village and gets the girl. He deserved her more than Ichabod, for while the scholar danced and counted his stuffed pigs, Brom experienced two human emotions; jealousy and love."

Chapter 8

HEADLESS!

The dominant spirit, however, that haunts this enchanted region, and seems to be commander-in-chief of all the powers of the air, is the apparition of a figure on horseback without a head. It is said by some to be the ghost of a Hessian trooper, whose head had been carried away by a cannon-ball, in some nameless battle during the revolutionary war; and who is ever and anon seen by the country folk hurrying along in the gloom of night, as if on the wings of the wind. His haunts are not confined to the valley, but extend at times to the adjacent roads, and especially to the vicinity of a church at no great distance...The body of the trooper, having been buried in the church-yard, the ghost rides forth to the scene of battle in nightly quest of his head; and that the rushing speed with which he sometimes passes along the Hollow, like a midnight blast, is owing to his being belated, and in a hurry to get back to the church-yard before daybreak (TLSH, 5).

Alas, poor Ichabod Crane! He coveted Katrina van Tassel's bounty more than her beauty. Thus a ruffian disguised as the Headless Horseman frightens the Yankee schoolmaster away in a Dutch-style charivari. A spirit dominant over Ichabod, Sleepy Hollow and current imaginations certainly holds all the powers of the air.

Scholars often assert that Washington Irving viewed his success and the lasting power of *The Legend* with the same perspective Baltus van Tassel had on his farm. "He was satisfied with his wealth, but not proud of it." They picture Irving's spirit looking over all the Headless Horseman movies,

Into Sleepy Hollow, 2008. *Photo by Todd Atteberry, www.thehistorytrekker.com.*

amusements, computer games, place names, sculptures and storytellers with amusement. Yet he just confesses to borrowing the tale from the oral tradition, not German folklore or a Revolutionary War journal. Years after *The Legend* was published, Irving suggested a source. Of course, he still maintained the shabby gentleman Diedrich Knickerbocker gathered the legend while visiting a dilapidated mill and reported back to Irving: "I verily believe it was to his [Diedrich's] conference with his African sage, and the precious revelations of the good dame of the spinning wheel, that we are indebted for the surprising though true history of Ichabod Crane and the headless horseman, which has since astounded and edified the world."

Confessing that he learned his most-famed tale from a humble pair from Sleepy Hollow makes for a charming story. A miller and spinner would certainly have many chances to gather and share local lore. Irving's revelation, however, rings true. Given the storied nature of both

Washington Irving and Sleepy Hollow, there are more tales to the making of the Headless Horseman.

Granted, Irving listened to tales from the many denizens of Sleepy Hollow. He also took to heart Jesse Merwin's charivari. He borrowed ideas found in Walter Scott's library of German and Scottish lore. The surprising truth is that there was a real headless Hessian!

The "Nameless" Battle of White Plains

Westchester County endured many skirmishes, raids, burnings and battles during the fight for independence from Great Britain. Thirty thousand men clashed in the swamps and on the hills at the Battle of White Plains, making it one of the biggest conflicts in the entire war. Size alone does not make White Plains the site of the "nameless battle" Washington Irving gives for the site of the Hessian's demise. The proof lies in the story of the battle itself.

George Washington's Continental army and militiamen suffered a bitter defeat on Long Island at the Battle of Brooklyn Heights. They managed a

Hessian's ford on the Bronx River, White Plains, New York, 2009. *Photo by Todd Atteberry, www.thehistorytrekker.com.*

clandestine escape to Manhattan thanks to the stealthy boatman of Colonel John Glover and with help from a timely windstorm. Tens of thousands of British troops, including several brigades from Germany, had arrived in the summer of 1776 to stop the rebellion. The British commander, General William Howe, looked for an opportunity to deliver a "sharp but not a serious blow" to the Americans. Sympathetic to their plight, Howe hoped to employ a show of force to frighten the wayward rebels to drop arms and negotiate peace. Consequently, he fought with the deliberation usually found in a game of chess.

Howe, for example, ordered a regiment of Hessian jaegers and grenadiers under Colonel von Donop to march up Manhattan to mop up the ragtag American militia. When Washington heard shots from his post in Harlem, he dashed down to take charge. He found his men dropping their weapons and fleeing in terror before the dreaded Hessians. Even experienced troops who had stood their ground months earlier at Bunker Hill in Boston high-tailed it when the Germans hit the Broadway. Some saw Washington lose his temper, claiming he struck retreating men with the back of his sword. Others say he froze in shock over his soldiers' cowardice. He barely escaped capture.

Later, Washington, along with a host of his best generals—Lee, Heath, Putnam, Sullivan, MacDougal, Spencer and Greene—decided to make a stand on the hilltops above a white misty pine swamp the Natives called Quarropas. Showing they would fight at the village of White Plains, they hoped to buy the American Revolution the precious time needed to hold off the British army.

On October 22, Israel Putnam manned Purdy Hill and Washington took the center line, with William Heath setting the right flank on Hatfield Hill. They made redoubts out of cornstalks, mud and high hopes. General Alexander MacDougal commanded Pennsylvanian backwoodsmen, while the Massachusetts fishermen dug in on a long ridge near Michael Chatterton's farm. The land belonged to the prominent Tory with a countryseat in Sleepy Hollow named Frederick Philipse.

On October 23, thousands of Hessians shipped up the Long Island Sound, landing at Davenport Neck to camp near the little French Huguenot and Quaker town of New Rochelle. Tales of Hessians bayoneting surrendering Americans at Brooklyn Heights spread throughout Westchester, proving not mere rumor. A British officer later described actions led by the German Count Von Donop: "Our Hessians and our brave Highlanders gave no quarter, and it was a fine sight to see with what alacrity they despatched the rebels with their bayonets."

Headless!

Whenever someone whispered, "Hessians coming!" they put out their home fires, drove off their cattle and hid their children. Conscripted soldiers on loan to King George III from Landgrave Frederick III of Hesse-Kassel, they made a fearsome impression upon their arrival. Glowering beneath brass miter caps held in place with chin strap just below sharp mustaches, they sported a long, swordlike hair queue. The Hessians prompted many horror stories. Some said these cruel mercenaries fought only for war booty. Others mixed up the straps with the mustaches to assert, "Hessians have two rows of teeth!" "Beware!' they warned. "If the 'Hushman' can't find food, he'll eat your children!" These were trying times in Westchester.

The German forces, under Colonel von Rall and General Heister, though not cannibals, intended to quash the contemptible American rebels. They resented their radical disrespect for authority. Howe needed to rein in the battle-eager Von Rall when they arrived at White Plains.

The British and Hessians assembled in a formidable force of about fourteen thousand men on October 28 at White Plains. An awestruck American captain, William Hull, wrote: "The approach of the British army. Its appearance was truly magnificent. A bright autumnal sun shed it's full luster on the polished arms; and the rich array of dress and military equipage gave an imposing grandeur to the scene, as they advanced in all the pomp and circumstances of war to give us battle."

General Howe let loose his Hessians on that brilliant autumn day. Von Rall's men charged Chatterton's hill, but seasoned Delaware soldiers under Colonel John Haslet's repelled them. While Howe deliberated, the angered Hessians fired their cannons. One of Haslet's men suffered a gory leg wound, frightening off some of the Minutemen in other units. Alexander MacDougal steadied his troops, but the Americans began to slip. Howe, at last, ordered a full assault. The British Seventeenth Dragoons under Alexander Leslie advanced on the American center. Colonels Von Rall and Donop attacked from the left and center. They forded the waist-deep Bronx River. The Hessians raced the skull and crossbones–wearing British dragoons to get a first shot at the rebels.

The woods on Chatterton Hill burned with cannon tow and spent paper bullet casings. Firing down, the Americans had managed to repel the first wave. A young captain Alexander Hamilton distinguished himself by keeping two small American cannons firing hotly. Rall drove his men to bayonet the Americans off the hill. Washington and his generals were forced to organize a hasty retreat. The Americans beat it back into North Castle.

General Sir Henry Clinton urged Howe to attack Washington's camps at night. Stung by an earlier ambush in Pelham where hundreds of Hessians fell in a "cowardly" attack from behind stone walls, Rall and Donop enthusiastically agreed. Howe rejected their plan as imprudent and out of character for a civilized army. They all agreed, though, on a big assault set for October 31. Fateful heavy rains changed this battle plan.

Howe instead sent an exploratory column of dragoons with Hessian artillery down the Connecticut Road, now Lake Street in White Plains. They learned of an American supply depot at Horton's Mill Pond, now Silver Lake. General William Heath stationed some artillery on the other side of the road near Merritt Hill. Apparently the Patriots had a resourceful captain like Alexander Hamilton keeping their powder dry. Here's what Heath wrote in his journal:

> *The artillery of the division was so well directed as to throw the British artillery-men several times into confusion. And finding that they could not here make any impression, drew back their pieces, the column not advancing. The British artillery now made a circuitous movement and came down toward the American right. Here, unknown to them were some 12 pounders; upon the discharge of which they made off with their field pieces as fast as their horses could draw them. A shot from the American cannon at this place took off the head of a Hessian artillery-man. They also left one of the artillery horses dead on the field. What other loss they sustained was not known.*

Thus, a Hessian on the battlefield at White Plains loses his head on Halloween! Other accounts show Americans heating their shot orange hot to scatter better, creating a pumpkinlike glowing projectile. Plus, according to believers in the supernatural, his spirit receives a ghost horse to ride. The following spring, American soldier and diarist Joseph Plumb Martin detailed the horror of finding "the bones of Hessians" scattered across the forlorn fields of White Plains. Bodies, especially if an officer's, occasionally got transported away from the field of battle for burial. The Old Dutch Church yard of Sleepy Hollow is about nine miles from White Plains.

THE HELPFUL HESSIAN

One local legend hints at a reason for burying the headless Hessian in Sleepy Hollow. Van Tassel cousins Peter and Cornelius lived on adjacent farms in Elmsford a few miles south of Sleepy Hollow. Finding King George's way of imposing taxes with an occupying army intolerable, the two rebelled. Declaring themselves American Patriots, they readied to fight in a militia band under Wolfert Acker. When the British fell to Gates and Arnold at Saratoga, they turned their attention to securing the land around New York City, especially Westchester County. Upon spying a British force patrolling near their homesteads, the cousins picked off several Redcoats from behind a stone wall. They escaped but not for long. Lieutenant Colonel Andreas Emmerick, an American Loyalist commander of dragoons, or horsemen, received orders on November 17, 1777, to punish the Van Tassels.

Commanding Hessian dragoons with a small contingent of Loyalist soldiers, they rode from the Bronx into the no-man's land of central Westchester. First, they burned down the tavern of Abraham Storms, a captain in Acker's militia. Next, they surrounded the Van Tassel farms and demanded surrender. The Van Tassels countered with a few rounds of musket shot. Enraged, Emmerick ordered his Hessians to burn the houses without granting the families the customary fifteen minutes to clear out belongings. The Hessians hastily obeyed. Setting the eaves to flame, they dashed in to drag out the Van Tassels as the king's prisoners. These poorly paid soldiers occasionally carried off whatever spoils of war they could grab from rebel houses.

Captured, the Van Tassel cousins saw their homes go up in flames. Hands tied, Emmerick forced the pair to drive their own cattle down to New York City to feed the king's army. The haze of war and smoke left Elizabeth van Tassel screaming. Two of her children remained in the burning house. Baby Leah slept in her cradle; clever Cornelius Jr. hid in his loft bedroom. Cornelius burst out of a shutter window to escape the heat and fire a musket. He leapt down into the looting soldiers, turning the gun into a swinging club. He knocked down a few Hessians and then fled. The teenage Cornelius escaped via an icy swim across the rushing Saw Mill River. He holed up on Beaver Mountain, one of those hills flanking Tarrytown.

Mrs. van Tassel braved the flames to search for her little daughter but staggered back out weeping in vain. One Hessian pitied her. He tore back through the blaze for the baby. He found the child and a quilted feather-stuffed blanket. The Hessian turned Elizabeth's tears to those of joy by presenting her with little Leah. Mother and child took refuge in a root cellar, while the helpful Hessian marched off empty handed. Feeling more pity, he had given the mother and child the quilt.

A distinguished Sleepy Hollow cemetery guide connects this Hessian's kindness to the headless Hessian. The Van Tassel family felt obligated to bury the latter after benefiting from the former. Naturally, the story is cited as the reason a decapitated foreign invader was laid to "rest" in the Old Dutch Church yard. The dates of each event, however, call into question this explanation. White Plains, as Irving's "nameless" battle, was fought in late October into early November 1776. Emmerick's raid occurred November 17, 1777.

There is still a way the grateful Elizabeth convinces the dominee of the Old Dutch Church to accept the headless Hessian for burial. There is nothing written by Washington Irving or primary sources stating when the headless Hessian got to the Old Dutch Church. Joseph Plumb Martin reported finding Hessian bones unburied around White Plains six months after the battle. Given the trying times in Westchester, the bones may have remained exposed in December 1777, when the Van Tassel cousins were released from prison. Elizabeth could have urged the men to then return the family a favor of a burial. A body interred without a head, without a marker, in the heart of a realm haunted by old Indian and German witch curses, remains a restless spirit to this day.

THE LITTLE MAN IN BLACK'S TALE

Washington Irving avidly collected stories of the American Revolution. Later he wrote an extensive biography of his namesake, George. One source of Irving's tales sprang forth from Aaron Burr. The Irving family always maintained friendship with the disgraced former vice president. Indeed, in 1825, Washington Irving even wrote a sympathetic story about the Little Man in Black who is unfairly branded a witch. His readers knew the darkened man was Burr.

Aaron Burr served as aide-de-camp to the "Old Wolf," General Israel Putnam, who fought with Heath and Washington at the Battle of White Plains. One of Putnam's militiamen from what is now Rockland County suffered a terrible fate. Abraham Onderdonk, according to a neighbor quoted in a Hackensack, New Jersey newspaper, "was killed by a cannon ball from the enemy separating his head from his shoulders." Surely this is the kind of incident Burr would share with a wide-eyed Washington Irving around long-stemmed pipes and brandy. Distinguished Irving biographer Andrew Burstein concurs. "It is not unreasonable to consider that Irving might have known the details" of this tale. Other scholars say Irving converted the headless patriotic American into a reviled Hessian for a more dramatic effect. Why base *The Legend* on a true tale gleaned from the Little Man in Black, when it is more reasonable to accept that Washington Irving read about the Hessian's decapitation in General Heath's 1798 published memoir?

Stories of headless soldiers floated in the gloomy Sleepy Hollow air when Irving first passed through in the 1790s. A documented account of a Hessian made headless on Halloween 1776 is the core of the kernel of *The Legend of Sleepy Hollow*. Add Jesse Merwin's charivari, scores of local curses, spells and ghost stories, and Washington Irving certainly has enough material for his 1818 epiphany crossing London Bridge. Another rich source, however, for the lore of the Headless Horseman of Sleepy Hollow needs some exploration.

German and Scottish Sources

The Wild Huntsmen

Henry "Nuncle" Brevoort received a revealing letter from his dear Lads of Kilkenny friend writing from England in May 1818. Washington Irving, while visiting with Scottish author Sir Walter Scott, wrote: "I have been some time past engaged in the study of the German language, and have got so far as to be able to read and splutter a little. It is a severe task…but the rich mine of German literature holds forth an abundant reward."

Washington Irving joined the craze then in Great Britain for all things German. Inspired by the "Deutsch," a year later Irving had his reliable pal Brevoort publish in New York the *Sketch Book*, including *The Legend of Sleepy Hollow*.

> *The Wild Huntsmen*
> *Be chased for ever through the wood;*
> *For ever roam the affrighted wild;*
> *And let thy fate instruct the proud,*
> *God's meanest creature is his child*

Walter Reichart, accounting for Irving's interest in German, wrote in the *New York Folklore Quarterly* that "Irving's enthusiasm for German literature and particularly for German romance and folklore was not fanned into a bright flame until his visit to Walter Scott." Washington's new friend and mentor turned him on to German works with his book *The Wild Huntsmen (aka The Chase)*. Scott translated it in 1796 from Gottfried August Burger's 1778 story *Die Wilde Jaeger*.

Burger possessed a passion for German *marchen*, a kind of fairy tale with humor and exaggeration. His *Die Wilde Jaeger* was an epic-styled poem based on the marchen "Wildgrave." The lore tells of Faulkenburgh, a fierce forest keeper, who lives only for the thrill of the chase. Even in death, his compulsion raises his spirit from the grave. People living near the dark forest always trembled at the sound of the Wildgrave's hunting horn and his baying dogs. A ghost-demon, he pursues his quarry, usually a stag, relentlessly through break and bramble, farm and village. Woe to those getting in the Wildgrave's way. He hurls putrid flesh! Faulkenburgh even dares shatter the sanctity of the Sabbath!

One young knight falls under the Wildgrave's spell. This nobleman, enthralled at the rush of the hunt, calls out to the Wildgrave, "Gluck zu Falkenburgh (Good luck to you)!" Once again, you must be careful for what you wish! This ghastly spook, cloaked and mounted on a fiery horse, rasps, "Dost thou wish me good sport?" Suddenly the young knight is caught in the spell of the Wildgrave's frenzied chase. Hounds baying, horn blasting, they crash into a hermit's church. There a monk utters a prayer. The Wildgrave's bones illuminate, but before vanishing, he cries, "Thou shalt share of the game!" The goblin hurls a piece of some rancid carcass at the young noble. Then,

> *'Twas hush'd:—One flash, of sombre glare,*
> *With yellow tinged the forests brown;*
> *Uprose the Wildgrave's bristling hair,*
> *And horror chill'd each nerve and bone*

Clearly Irving's Headless Horseman follows the Wild Huntsmen's lead. When the headless Hessian disappears, he "turned into a skeleton springs away over the tree-tops with a clap of thunder vanish in a flash of fire." A goblin also brains Crane with some strange fleshy thing. *The Legend* too has a prayer offering as a way to ward off the demon. It just doesn't work because the schoolmaster is too scared to sing his ghost-busting psalm. Irving explains, "His parched tongue clove to the roof of his mouth, and he could not utter a stave."

Headless!

The galloping Hessian rides on, 1893 illustration. *By George Boughton for* Rip Van Winkle *and* The Legend of Sleepy Hollow *by Washington Irving.*

Reichart, a meticulous researcher of all things German in Washington Irving, discovered another source of the Sleepy Hollow Horseman. Irving's alter ego, Geoffrey Crayon, searches among the papers of Diedrich Knickerbocker to find *The Legend of Sleepy Hollow*. Reichart found Irving's bookstore receipt as proof of the German influence. It listed a 1791 book called *Legenden von Rubenzahl* by J.C.A. Musaus. Irving's clever tongue naturally stuck to the roof of his mouth when asked whether he borrowed from the Germans. Discovering, then, the story pattern, along with a few closely rewritten passages floated from Musaus into *The Legend*, reveals much of the Headless Horseman's origins.

Number-Nip V

Number-Nip V appears in *Legenden von Rubenzahl* as a kind of mischievous imp, not unlike those encountered above the Tappan Zee. A denizen of the mysterious forests of Germany, he plays trickster to local notables on their adventures. Here, Number-Nip V disguises himself as a headless goblin to seek revenge on an obnoxious party of nobles and a flappable fellow named John. Out in the wilderness on a carriage ride, away from the "snug security of Breslaw," they encounter a peculiar apparition:

> *John…saw, to his utter confusion, stalking on about a stone's throw before the coach, a jet-black figure, of a size exceeding that of a man, crowned with a broad Spanish tippet: but what was the most suspicious circumstance in this whole appearance, was its being without an head. If the coach halted, the figure drove on* [and] *it proceeded also.*

Here's Irving's similar passage from *The Legend*: "In the dark shadow of the grove, in the margin of the brook, he beheld something huge, misshapen and towering. It stirred not but seemed to be gathering up the gloom, like some gigantic monster ready to spring upon the traveler."

Ichabod makes the same mistake the young nobleman does in *Die Wilde Jaeger* by accosting a goblin. "Who are you?" True to the tradition, this sets off the wild chase, with the halts and starts to shake off the goblin, found in *Legenden von Rubenzahl* and in *The Legend*. Musaus slips in humor more overtly than does Irving:

Headless!

"Who's there? What is all that noise for?"

"Your honour," replied John with a trembling voice, "Be so good as only just to look out the window; for, Lord have mercy upon us! There walks a man without a head close beside us!"

"Blockhead as thou art," replied the Countess, "Of what is thy vulgar imagination dreaming? And if that was the case," continues she in a tone of raillery, "A man without an head is no rarity; there are plenty in Breslaw and other places."

Sleepy Hollow, to be sure, is one of those other places. Indeed, "Gotham," the nickname Washington Irving gave to New York City for its heedless hectic people, is yet another. Thus, the stage is set for the full sighting of each story's monster. They first attempt to ward off the creature with prayer. Recall Ichabod trying to sing his protective psalm. The idea occurs here in Musuas's tale: "John fortified himself with all the prayers he knew against evil sprits; with a long string of pater-nosters and benedicites into the bargain, reeking all the time with a cold sweat."

The pattern of a fits and starts pursuit with an emergence from the shadows again is set by Musuas and followed by Irving. Here Number-Nip V, disguised as the headless goblin, is discovered by John:

The black figure, that had disappeared for a few moments out of John's view, emerged from among the bushes, and advanced towards the road. It was now plain to be seen that John's eye had taken a false measure—the man on foot had an head as well as other people, only he did not wear it, according to the usual fashion, between his shoulders, but carried it under his arm, just as if it had been a lap-dog.

Washington Irving uses the same device to bring his monster out of the brush and shadows. Granted, Number-Nip V is on foot rather than horseback. Note the same reference to the shoulders in each passage:

On mounting a rising ground, which brought his fellow-traveller in relief against the sky, gigantic in height and muffled in a cloak, Ichabod was horror-struck on perceiving that he was headless! But his horror was still more increased on observing that the head which should have rested on his shoulders, was carried on the pommel of his saddle (TLSH, 65)!

The headless Hessian's chase of Ichabod Crane takes inspiration from the earlier Wildgrave story. Irving, however, gives a more dramatic race. His is indeed another wild haunt, one rich with tangible images. The saddle breaks. Ichabod clutches Gunpowder until "he verily feared would cleave him asunder!" This scene ignited the imaginations of master painters like Washington Allston and John Quidor.

When Musaus's goblin readies to deliver the coup de grace, John first attempts to give the proper greeting. The ghoul interrupts like Wildgrave, hurling a fleshy projectile:

> *John, against whom the formidable figure in the black seemed to be meditating some design, began, in the anguish of his heart, the salutation appointed to be addressed to all good sprits, but before he could speak it out the monster took his head from under his arm, and hurled it at John: it stuck him right on the forehead, and the blow was so severe that he tumbled headlong from the box over the fore-wheel.*

Once again Irving finds this way a useful template:

> *Ichabod cast a look behind to see if his pursuer should vanish, according to rule, in a flash of fire and brimstone. Just then he saw the goblin rising in his stirrups, and in the very act of hurling his head at him. Ichabod endeavored to dodge the horrible missile, but too late. It encountered his cranium with a tremendous crash—he was tumbled headlong into the dust, and Gunpowder, the black steed, and the goblin rider, passed by like a whirlwind* (TLSH, 68).

Musaus goes for the immediacy of comic relief to end his scene: "The mask and drapery were presently stripped away, and out there came a well-proportioned curly-pated fellow…he doubted not but the horseman was Number-Nip himself."

Irving masterfully exits his goblin and Ichabod into the mists of Sleepy Hollow. Their spirits disperse, leaving us to wonder. We are left still haunted today.

Tam O'Shanter

Irving borrowed another page from a book of wonder found on the shelves of Sir Walter's library. The Doon River Kirk Bridge proves most daunting to the chasing ghoul in *Tam O'Shanter*. The epic poem, written in 1791 by the bard of Scotland, Robert Burns, features a hen-pecked fellow beguiled by his landlord's wife and a comely witch wearing nothing but a "cutty-sark." Tam, hotly pursued by that witch, urges his horse to cross over the Doon at a stone bridge, hard by the ruinous Alloway Church.

Supernatural spirits shun water crossings. Apparently they fear any stream could become the River Styx. Cross it, and Hades will snatch your wayward soul to hold forever. Desperate to catch Tam, the witch lunges, but Tam and most of his horse, Meg, have gotten across. All she manages to catch of Tam, before vanishing, is his horse's tail. The remaining stub gave rise to a certain style of cap known as the tam-o'-shanter.

Irving follows the tradition of escaping a ghost at a church bridge with an accuracy sure to please the poets of old. Before he gets his ghost to blaze, however, there's the proverbial ride through purgatory. Burns set Tam on the path that the frightful Ichabod would follow. They both pass through their own little odysseys of grim and ghostly sites:

> *Alloway's Church was drawing near,*
> *Where ghosts and owls nightly cry.*
> *By this time he was across the ford,*
> *Where in the snow the peddler got smothered;*
> *And past the birch trees and the huge stone,*
> *Where drunken Charlie broke his neck bone;*
> *And through the thorns, and past the monument,*
> *Where hunters found the murdered child;*
> *And near the thorn, above the well,*
> *Where Mungo's mother hung herself.*
> *Before him the river Doon pours all his floods.*

Wildgrave tramples poor peasants, their cows, their churches and anything in their way, creating the same sort of sorrowful passage. Following Katrina van Tassel's rejection of the schoolmaster's marriage proposal, he must travel through the forlorn night on a sway-backed, one-eyed horse. Here's a touch of Ichabod's descent into the ghost realm of Wiley's Swamp:

> *A few rough logs, laid side by side, served for a bridge over this stream. On that side of the road where the brook entered the wood, a group of oaks and chestnuts, matted thick with wild grape-vines, threw a cavernous gloom over it. To pass this bridge was the severest trial. It was at this identical*

spot that the unfortunate Andre was captured, and under the covert of those chestnuts and vines were the sturdy yeomen concealed who surprised him. This has ever since been considered a haunted stream, and fearful are the feelings of the school-boy who has to pass it alone after dark (TLSH, 62).

Irving lines up a local cast of spooks to match Burns's "smothered peddler" and "murdered child." Ichabod has to run a gauntlet of ghosts. He passed a tree with an eerie resemblance to the specter of the White Lady of Raven Rock. The "unfortunate Andre," of course, refers to the hanged British officer turned spy. Ichabod missed that ghost's wailings. They mark the appalling passageway to the scary chase. Here Irving's not stealing from the Scottish and German bards but just tipping his hat to them. They all follow a timeless ghost-story tradition. You don't just bump into the principal spirit. Ancient poets like Homer and Dante foretold of the harrowing journey necessary before the descent to the darkest realm.

The odyssey to the dark side transforms. Ichabod's turned into a ghost or, worse, a city lawyer. One final tale found by Reichart "among the papers" of Washington Irving also hints at the thrill, chill and relief felt after an encounter with Sleepy Hollow's headless wonder.

The Headless Horseman chases Ichabod, illustration. *By George Boughton for* Rip Van Winkle *and* The Legend of Sleepy Hollow *by Washington Irving*

The Headless Grey Huntsman

The old frau knew she had strayed too far from Dresden when she found herself recalling her grandfather.

He always warned: never wander to where you cannot smell the hearth fires! Now she smelled only the oaks, shading the glen at Lost Waters. Working quickly to fill her basket with acorns, she felt a chill.

Next, a shrill hunting horn broke the thick air. The old frau stood up. There was a thrashing in the forest—falling branches accompanied the trumpet blasts.

She crouched behind a tree trunk. A great grey horse brayed. She peered out and caught a look at the rider. Hidden in a flowing grey cape, she gasped, "The headless hunter!"

She noticed his spurred boots, bow and head.

"I pray for the one he murdered! I pray for this one who had to lose his head!"

The headless grey huntsman reined in. The old frau froze. Then he resumed riding by Lost Waters.

The old frau spilled out her acorns and slipped back to where the smoke scented the air. There she began collecting nuts again while counting her blessings.

Chapter 9

THE STORYTELLER

*There is no encouragement for ghosts in most of our villages, for they have
scarcely had time to finish their first nap and turn themselves in their graves,
before their surviving friends have traveled away from the neighborhood; so that
when they turn out at night to walk their rounds, they have no acquaintance left to
call upon. This is perhaps the reason why we so seldom hear of ghosts except in
our long-established Dutch communities (TLSH, 52).*

STORYTELLERS

Diedrich Knickerbocker, Geoffrey Crayon and Washington Irving together
gathered the stories found within *The Legend of Sleepy Hollow*. Indeed, we
hear of ghosts rising from Native lore, Dutch American customs, traditional
German tales, Revolutionary War journals and, ultimately, Irving's
imagination. Our storyteller's perspective on all these sources colors the lore
of *The Legend*.

Edwin Burrows and Mike Wallace comment in their tome *Gotham*:
"Indeed Irving's *History* can be read as one long screed, tempered somewhat
by comparing them to a fictive Dutch Golden Age when every thing was
better than it has ever been since." People travel in and away from the
neighborhood of Sleepy Hollow with such frightening frequency that they
misunderstand those ghosts of "Golden" times. Again, Judith Richardson
says that this is precisely why spirits crowd into the consciousness today:
"The area's hauntings emanate from social and historical tensions created

by a rapid pace of development and obsolescence." The storyteller of Sleepy Hollow, longing for the old dream of the Hudson Valley, emerges from the hustle and bustle of change to recall for us the old stories. He carries us back to an earlier age, but it is a contrived scene.

Diedrich Knickerbocker, that storyteller with a significant name, stepped out from the dream into the busy streets of New York first as a shrewd publicity stunt. An advertisement appeared in 1809 New York newspapers just before the publishing of Washington Irving's *History of New-York*. It requested help locating "a shabby looking gentlemen" who had left a sheaf of writings of that title in a hotel. Irving succeeded in piquing interest in his coming book while putting forth a vision of himself in the future. "Died Rich Knicker Booker," as biographer Burnstein notes, seems to refer to a wealthy fellow nodding off cozy among his old books. Granted, Irving knew a real Congressman Herman Knickerbocker but selected the name to help tell his nostalgic tales.

Historic Hudson Valley's *Legend of Sleepy Hollow* storyteller Jonathan Kruk, 2009. *Photo by Todd Atteberry, www.thehistorytrekker.com.*

Geoffrey Crayon seems to causally happen upon Knickerbocker's manuscript while ostensibly just out to make some written "sketches" on the Hudson Valley. He downplays *The Legend of Sleepy Hollow* as just another chronicle. All the influences from German, Scottish and other sources are hidden in these found papers. The old saw then sounds against Washington Irving as a copycat, stealing the story from Musaus and others. The great New York folklorist Harold W. Thompson, in his book *Body Boots and Britches*, reminds, "Irving did not need to visit Germany—which he did two years after writing the Sketch Book—nor must we suppose that he was just introduced to German Legends in Sir Walter Scott's library. He could have heard plenty of German as well as Dutch legends along the Hudson."

OTHER HEADLESS HORSEMEN IN NEW YORK

Irving, indeed, heard many other tales too along the Hudson. A few significant standouts prove the air changes in the lower Hudson Valley with the spirits still abounding between the layers. New York holds a surfeit of decapitated spirits, which may have filtered into Irving's ever-active imagination. Louis C. Jones, the master-collector of New York lore, in the 1940s reports a tale from the Schenevus Valley of the Catskills.

Withering Hans

Once upon a time, Hans was a shafer, tougher than a catamount and so Dutch that he had sauerkraut hanging out of his ears. Always he'd be the first to leap up to help and the last to stop flirting with the ladies. When out came the roasting apples, long pipes and longer tales of the Catskill ghosts and witches, Hans laughed, where everyone else jumped.

One yarn of a headless revolutionary rider filled him with the biggest doubt. Folks told that this ghost casts spells over those who crossed his spooking path. Hans listened to all of it and declared over and over, "I'd like to meet the Headless Rider some day. I'll trade him my own head for a loaf of bread."

Careless Hans got what he wished for! A day of horror came! Sauntering along a wooded track one evening, Hans met up with the Headless Rider. Our sturdy fellow became nervous as a cat with wet feet. He could not speak, let alone make and jest about trading his head for bread!

When Hans returned to Schenevus, he had an "unknowing, unseeing" look in his sky-blue eyes. Folks found poor Hans's mind just withered away after encountering that Headless Rider.

Crawbucky Hessians

This is one of several legends told by the old-timers on various occasions in the Crawbucky Fish House, to while away the hours before hauling in the seine. Legends had been handed down father to son in Westchester County. Washington Irving undoubtedly founded his Legend of Sleepy Hollow *from just the same source (*The Crawbucky Tales, *1920).*

Croton on Hudson, with its storied Teller's Point, lies about ten miles north of Sleepy Hollow. Major Andre planned to rendezvous with the British warship, *The Vulture,* until a couple Patriots chased it off with a cannon they dragged to Crawbucky Beach. Fishermen there swapped quite a few yarns known as the *Crawbucky Tales.* They illuminate close calls with witches, a fiery señorita, devilish fires and treasure hidden at Money Hill by the privateer turned pirate William Kidd. One curious adventure takes Uncle Ben out rowing for a pot of money spied just floating near the point. Whenever the fishermen get near the loot, it blazes before vanishing like the Headless Horseman at the bridge by the Old Dutch Church. Among the *Revolutionary Yarns* is an account of the Hessian foragers. Following the Battle of White Plains, they strayed upon Teller's Point, scrounging for food. A fellow known as Rifle Jake led a party of Patriots in apprehending the "long toothed" Germans. They decided to punish stealing soldiers by forcing them to eat all they had swiped. Bread, pie, cookies, cabbages and all went down the Hessians' hatches at gunpoint. Just when the Germans felt they'd burst, they begged for mercy. Jake took them all as prisoners.

One Hessian lingers to haunt Croton on Hudson. Schoolchildren over one hundred years ago began reporting a headless Hessian in uniform riding on Mount Airy Road. Others swear he strays as far away as Hanover Street, a road in Yorktown with a name left over from the days of King George. A few maintain it's the ghost of one of the over-stuffed Germans from Crawbucky Beach, head tucked beneath his collar from embarrassment. Of course, he may simply have been the decapitated artilleryman seeking his head from Sleepy Hollow.

Headless in Yonkers

High above the rolling heights of Yonkers on Valentine Hill is Saint Joseph's Seminary. Around the turn of the last century, many Poles and Italians migrated to that city on the Hudson. They needed one of those reminders from days gone past. A horrid specter with a bloody neck stump roved about the neighborhood, doubtlessly moving many to prayer. A Cow-Boy caught in the area by vengeful rebels may have taken the unfortunate thief's head, leaving him to haunt the newcomers to Yonkers.

Jug o' Rum!

Again, this headless tale occurred in the late 1890s south of Fishkill, the big supply depot for the Americans during the Revolution. This tale, collected in the early 1960s by Nelson DeLanoy of the Putnam County Historical Society, recounts a local legend of a ghost pig connected to another thief who lost his head. Washington Irving frequently visited Cold Spring on Hudson, the destination of the one who became known as "Vinegar Pete" following this ghost encounter.

Pete had gone courting a young woman in Fishkill. Heading home in a horse-drawn cart to Cold Spring late at night proves a harrowing trip when traversing the dreaded Dry Bridge near the old Haight House on Albany Post Road. The story of a soldier who lost his head in a fight with another over a stolen pig filled the air in those days when night fell. Pete found his head heavy as his heart, especially after his sweetheart scorned his marriage offer. Wending toward the bridge, Pete felt relieved when the headless soldier failed to show up to haunt. Then something grunted and leaped into Pete's cart. He couldn't see it, but the squeals and unearthly grunts let the poor fellow know that he had the soldier's pilfered porker as a riding companion.

The animal goblin struck fear in Pete and his horse. The latter mad dashed all the way down toward the 1867-built Baptist Church. Weird foxfire flashes accompanied them. Pete was bone jangled and trembling when words took shape.

"Jug o' rum! Jug o' rum!" The spirit chanted until Pete pulled out the drink he carried to fortify himself from under the seat. Heaving it to send the ghost after the jug, Pete cried, "'Tis not! It's vinegar!"

Today's Headless Horseman, 2011 watercolor ink. *Ian Devaney.*

Perhaps it was the rum or the presence of the church, but there at the old Cold Spring Carmel turnpike the ghost pig vanished. Naturally when the tale got repeated, everyone soon said it all happened to Vinegar Pete. The Dry Bridge has been removed; the road straightened by the headless soldier's ghost pig rides on.

Farther north, and across the river near Sharon, rides still another ghost horseman. This spirit takes an extraordinary form. Apparently a horse with fiery hooves, head and eyes, its body is composed of the human rider. He rides bareback, of course, leaving burn marks on the ground and fear in hearts when he crosses paths. Headless Horsemen ride with some regularity in a few other locales in New York. Reports from Columbia County of a Headless Horseman come from few sources beyond Jesse Merwin's charivari by Brom van Alstyne. A few headless Revolutionary ghosts stray in nearby New Jersey, but above all, the Headless Horseman of Sleepy Hollow reigns as commander in chief.

Today's Horseman

Other communities, from the shores of the Hudson to Hollywood, contribute to the myriad manifestations of the galloping Hessian today. Thousands visit Sleepy Hollow for that authentic Halloween experience. Philipseburg Manor, a site managed by Historic Hudson Valley, bases its October weekends on *The Legend*. People come for the gory "Horseman's Hollow" and the enchanting "Pumpkin Blaze" at Van Cortlandt Manor, and dramatic retellings of *The Legend of Sleepy Hollow* are performed at the Old Dutch Church. A popular haunted hayride farther north in Ulster County uses the Headless Horseman name to help draw tens of thousands every autumn.

Disney World features a Headless Horseman rider and storyteller, freely adapting *The Legend* in a pared-down version that gallops around the famed amusement site.

Uncanny Tales Comics featured a *Sleepy Hollow* story in 1954 and introduced a Headless Horseman character in 1999, the same year the film *Sleepy Hollow* was released. The blockbuster by Tim Burton, starring Johnny Depp as investigator Ichabod Crane, grossed over $200 million.

Earlier movies include a 1922 silent version starring Will Rogers as Ichabod, a 1948 Disney production with Bing Crosby and a 1980 film with Jeff Goldblum and Dick Butkus. Shelley Duval produced a short version, and

Glenn Close narrates another for Rabbit Ears Radio. The 1944 horror film *The Curse of the Cat People* relies on the Headless Horseman to terrify a little girl.

Headless Horseman characters appear in many computer games, including the highly popular World of Warcraft.

An avant-garde band called the Headless Horseman offers an eclectic sound of Icelandic folk songs with a New York edge.

Sleepy Hollow and Tarrytown, New York, share a local high school with the Headless Horseman as their mascot. Students reportedly dare one another to visit the Old Dutch Church Cemetery, where the Horseman occasionally rides around midnight.

Valatie, New York, just outside of Kinderhook, salutes Jesse Merwin with an entire Ichabod Crane School District. Their mascot, rather like the one at Sleepy Hollow High, is a headless rider.

Conner Prairie, Indiana, an interactive history park, follows the current model of shying away from a full Headless Horseman story, opting for "skeletons, witches and ghosts trying to warn you about the infamous Headless Horseman."

There's a Sleepy Hollow in Illinois and California, plus a number of subdivisions too. Finally, there are Headless Horseman costumes for dogs.

THE WHOLE PLACE STILL ABOUNDS WITH SPIRITS

Today, Sleepy Hollow boasts a cornucopia of spirits. Thirty years ago, local high school students determined that ghosts continued to favor this drowsy, dreamy land. The tales they unearthed in the great oral tradition include dozens that Washington Irving could weave into his works. Here is a sampling of current spooks in Sleepy Hollow:

- The Bronze Lady of Sleepy Hollow Cemetery sits in repose before a mausoleum. If someone sits in her lap, spits in her eye, kicks her shin, knocks on her tomb and looks in, nightmares will plague you for two weeks!
- An assortment of apartment houses all situated in what once was Wiley's Swamp is haunted by ghosts of deceased war veterans, murdered people and a Lady in Black.
- Further, the golf course on the other side of the cemetery features an impish spirit, interfering with putts and stringing together streaks of curses.

- The woods near the course hold a great hairy Bigfoot-like creature. He once reportedly twisted a pair of dropped hunting rifles around a tree.
- And, of course, on dark nights, the galloping Hessian's horse's hooves may be heard beneath and nearby the current cemetery bridge. The Headless Horseman continues to tramp by the old one, though it no longer stands for us mortals.

No More North Tarrytown

Travel writers, on the web especially, lament the lack of ghost savvy among Sleepy Hollowers. Conducting informal surveys, few folks in restaurants or on the street right across from the famed Horseman crossing bridge could identify the galloping Hessian, let along poor Ichabod. A 2006 installation of a fantastic metal sculpture of Ichabod and the Horseman apparently draws blanks or "a picture of horse and buggy days" when locals were asked to answer, "What is this work of art?"

In 1997, North Tarrytown's Chamber of Commerce, reeling from the closure of a General Motors plant, spearheaded a movement to reestablish a connection to the region's principal spirit. Recognizing the way Washington Irving put the Hudson Valley on the map in the early 1800s, the chamber convinced the village to change its name to Sleepy Hollow. The chamber succeeded, but many cling proudly to North Tarrytown, sporting bumper stickers showing they are its residents. Tourism, thanks to Historic Hudson Valley, a parade and continued fascination with the Headless Horseman, grows in Sleepy Hollow.

Dark Shadows

Once upon a time, Thom Wolke, a local impresario concert creator, decided to link together two highly popular local legends. *The Legend of Sleepy Hollow* and *Dark Shadows* share a common bond in Tarrytown. Washington Irving's story, of course, is set in the village "where farmers have a tendency to tarry in the tavern." The nearby estate of Lyndhurst served as a location for the 1960s television "spook-opera" series *Dark Shadows*. The Old House of Collinwood still garners attention from devoted fans. The possibilities of a "vampire meets Headless Horseman" extravaganza sent Wolke howling at the moon with fiendish joy.

Road sign: Headless Horseman Xing, 2009. *Photo by Todd Atteberry, www.thehistorytrekker.com.*

In the early 1990s, Wolke secured the Old Dutch Church for a complete unabridged reading of *The Legend of Sleepy Hollow* by aging Canadian actor Jonathan Frid. He portrayed the *Dark Shadows* vampire Barnabus Collins in the late '60s. The concert sold out. He gave a chillingly dramatic reading of *The Legend.*

One final surprise shocked the audience when a braying horse, complete with a headless rider, galloped right up to the church window, leering. Frid lost his cool and shrieked like a ghost!

THE GOOD SPIRIT

The Legend, along with the equally enchanting story *Rip Van Winkle,* continues to enchant all as films, books, plays, ballets, operas, videos and games. One unusual source on the storyteller's perspective comes from the mother of one of Washington Irving's crushes. Mrs. Amelia Foster wrote about the author to a friend: "He looks upon life as a picture, but to catch its beauties, its lights—not its defects and shadows."

Washington Irving wrote in vivid pictures of Sleepy Hollow's spirit stories. Today the enduring shadow and beauty found in the Headless Horseman give the author's ghost a laugh, leading us to suspect he knows more about the matter than he chose to tell.

Irving, writing in 1843 about his homestead of Sunnyside, said, "I really believe that when I die I shall haunt it: but it will be as a good spirit, that no one needs be afraid of."

BIBLIOGRAPHY

Arrowsmith, Nancy, and George Moorse. *A Field Guide to the Little People.* New York: Hill and Wang, 1977.

Axelrod, Alan. *The Real History of the American Revolution.* New York: Sterling Pub, 2007.

Bacon, Edgar M. *Chronicles of Tarrytown and Sleepy Hollow.* New York: G.P. Putnam's Sons, 1897.

Bailey, Henry D.B. *Local Tales and Historical Sketches.* Fishkill Landing, NY: John W. Spaight, Fishkill Standard Office, 1874.

Boyle, T. Coraghessan. *World's End.* New York: Viking, 1987.

Briggs, Katharine. *An Encyclopedia of Fairies.* New York: Pantheon Books, 1976.

Burrows, Edwin, and Mike Wallace. *Gotham: A History of New York City to 1898.* New York: Oxford Press, 1999.

Burstein, Andrew. *The Original Knickerbocker: The Life of Washington Irving.* New York: Basic Books, 2007.

Carmer, Carl. *The Hudson.* New York: Farrar & Rinehart Inc., 1939.

Clyne, Patricia Edwards. *Hudson Valley Faces and Places.* Woodstock, NY: Overlook Press, Peter Mayer Publishers, Inc., 2005.

———. *Hudson Valley Tales and Trails.* Woodstock, NY: Overlook Press, Peter Mayer Publishers, Inc., 1990.

Dorland, Mrs. Jack A. "Was Hulda Witch or Heroine?" *Tarrytown Daily News,* March 28, 1975.

Duboc, Jesse. *In the Days of Ichabod.* Ann Arbor, MI: Edward Brothers, 1939.

Fabend, Firth Haring. *A Dutch Family in the Middle Colonies, 1660–1800.* New Brunswick, NJ: Rutgers University Press, 1991.

Funk, Elisabeth Paling. "Washington Irving and His Dutch-American Heritage." Unpublished manuscript, private collection.

Goodman, Edward C. *Hudson River Valley Reader*. Kennebunkport, ME: Cider Mill Press, 2008.

Hargreaves, Reginald, and Lewis Melville. *Great German Short Stories*. New York: Boni and Liveright, 1929

Hatch, Robert McConnell. *Major John Andre: A Gallant in Spy's Clothing*. Boston: Houghton Mifflin Company, 1986.

Hellman, George S. *Washington Irving, Esquire*. New York: Alfred A. Knopf, 1925.

Hoffman, Daniel G. "Irving's Use of American Folklore in *The Legend of Sleepy Hollow*." *PMLA* 68 (June 1953).

Hufeland, Otto. *Westchester County during the American Revolution, 1775–1783*. Harrison, NY: Harbor Hill Books, 1982.

Hunt, Freeman. *Letters about the Hudson River and Its Vicinity*. New York: Freeman Hunt Publishing, 1837.

Hutchinson, Lucille, and Theodore Hutchinson. *The Centennial History of North Tarrytown*. N.p.: Historical Society of the Tarrytowns Serving Sleepy Hollow and Tarrytown, 1975.

Irving, Washington. *Diedrich Knickerbocker's History of New-York*. Tarrytown, NY: Sleepy Hollow Press, 1981.

———. *The Legend of Sleepy Hollow*. New York: G.P. Putnam's Son, 1899.

———. *Stories of the Hudson*. Harrison, NY: Harbor Hill Books, 1984.

Jones, Louis C. *Things That Go Bump in the Night*. New York: Hill and Wang, 1939.

Kalm, Peter. *Peter Kalm's Travels in North America*. New York: Dover Publications Inc., 1937.

Kingston, Cecelia, ed. *Folklore of the Tarrytowns*. Unpublished manuscript, 1979. Historical Society of the Tarrytowns Serving Sleepy Hollow and Tarrytown.

Lederer, Richard M., Jr. *The Place Names of Westchester County*. Harrison, NY: Harbor Hill Books, 1978.

Lippard, George. *Washington and His Generals, or Legends of the Revolution*. Philadelphia: G.B. Zieber & Company, 1847.

Lossing, Benson J. *The Hudson: From the Wilderness to the Sea*. Hensonville, NY: Black Dome Press Corporation, 2000.

Martin, J.P. *Private Yankee Doodle*. Hallowell, ME: 1830.

Mayo, Gretchen Will. *Star Tales*. New York: Walker and Company, 1987.

Meeske, Harrison. *The Hudson Valley Dutch and Their Houses*. New York: Purple Mountain Press, 1998.

Musaus, Johann Carl A. *Popular Tales of the Germans V1 (1791)*. London: J. Murray, 1796.

Neider, Charles. *Complete Tales of Washington Irving*. New York: Da Capo Press, Inc., 1975.

Pritchard, Evan T. *Estuaries and Algonquins*. N.p.: self-published, 2000.

———. *Native New Yorkers*. San Francisco, CA: Council Oak Books, 2005.

Reichart, Walter A. "Washington Irving's Interest in German Folklore." *New York Folklore* (Autumn 1957).

Richardson, Judith. *Possessions: The History and Uses of Haunting in the Hudson Valley*. Cambridge, MA: Harvard University Press, 2003.

Rinaldi, Thomas E., and Robert J. Yasinsac. *Hudson Valley Ruins*. Hanover, NH: University Press of New England, 2006.

Rodes, Sara Puryear. "Washington Irving's Uses of Traditional Folklore." *New York Folklore* (Spring 1957).

Schlosser, S.E. *Spooky New York*. Guilford, CT: The Globe Pequot Press, 2005.

Shattuck, Martha Dickinson. *Explores Fortunes and Love Letters: A Window on New Netherland*. Albany, NY: New Netherland Institute, 2009.

Shonnard, Frederic, and W.W. Sponner. *History of Westchester County*. New York: New York History Company, 1900.

Skinner, Charles M. *Myths and Legends of Our Own Land*. Philadelphia: J.B. Lippincot Company, 1896.

Smith, David. *New York 1776: The Continental's First Battle*. New York: Esprey Publishing Ltd., 2008.

Swanson, Susan Cochran. *Between the Lines*. Pelham, NY: The Junior League of Pelham, Inc., 1975.

Venables, Robert W. *The Hudson Valley in the American Revolution*. Albany: New York State, 1975.

Walsh, John Evangelist. *The Execution of Major Andre*. New York: Palgrave, 2001.

Zehner, John R. *Crisis in the Lower Hudson Valley*. New York: Rockland Instant Copy, 1995.

Relevant Websites

Columbia County Historical Society, www.cchsny.org.

Friends of the Old Dutch Church and Burying Ground, www.olddutchburyingground.org/sleepy_country.html.

Highland Studio, www.thehighlandstudio.com.

Historic Hudson Valley, www.hudsonvalley.org.

Infanterie Regiment von Donop, www.vondonop.org.

"Livingston-Svirsky Archive (LiSA)." Alice Curtis Desmond & Hamilton Fish Library. dfl.highlands.com/lisa.html.

Love's Guide to the Church Bells of the City of London, london.lovesguide.com.

Military and Historical Image Bank, www.historicalimagebank.com.

MuseumsUSA.org, "The Historical Society, Inc. Serving Sleepy Hollow and Tarrytown, Tarrytown NY," www.museumsusa.org/museums/info/1154921.

Putnam County Historical Society and Foundry School Museum, www.pchs-fsm.org.

Rich Bala, Folk Balladeer, www.richbala.com.

Sleepy Hollow Chamber of Commerce, www.sleepyhollowchamber.com.

Todd Atteberry.com, www.thehistorytrekker.com.

U.S. History.org, http://www.ushistory.org.

ABOUT THE AUTHOR

Born in El Paso, Texas, but raised in Westchester County, New York, Jonathan Kruk grew up on tall tales and daydreams. He toured the country in a 1968 Volkswagen Beetle, watered Henry Kissinger's office plants and regaled his rambunctious brothers with bedtime "boojzhak" tales.

Jonathan made storytelling his full-time career in 1989. Every year, he performs for thousands of children at hundreds of schools, libraries and historic sites in the Hudson Valley and metropolitan New York. He engages children with finger fables and fairy-tale theater and as a medieval troubadour. Every October, Kruk's performances of *The Legend of Sleepy Hollow* for Historic Hudson Valley sell out. An Early Stages teaching artist, Kruk brings stories of colonial and Revolutionary times to New York City schoolchildren. He performs traditional stories and songs with Rich Bala as the Hudson River Ramblers.

His recordings of *The Legend of Sleepy Hollow*, *Rip Van Winkle*, *The Rainbow Dragon*, *Barkface & Rootnose*, *Halloween Tales*, *Revolution on the River* and *Once Upon the Hudson* have won Parent's Choice awards and NAPPA honors. He was selected in 2008 as Best Storyteller in the Hudson Valley. The National Society of the Sons of the American Revolution presented Kruk with the Citizenship Medal. He is also an Eagle Scout.

Jonathan's Sleepy Hollow work has been featured on the Travel and History Channels. He's performed at Pete Seegers's Clearwater Festival, New York's Quadricentenial, the New-York Historical Society and for thirty *Magic Tours in Tales of Elfin Lands* at Pound Ridge Reservation.

Jonathan lives in a cottage in the Hudson Highlands with his wife, actress and filmmaker Andrea Sadler. For more information, go to his website, www.jonathankruk.com.

Visit us at
www.historypress.net

CPSIA information can be obtained
at www.ICGtesting.com
Printed in the USA
LVHW020248141120
671367LV00001B/52